The Connected Apple Family

Discover the Rich Apple Ecosystem of the
Mac, **iPhone**, **iPad**, and **AppleTV**

JEFF CARLSON and DAN MOREN

PEACHPIT PRESS

The Connected Apple Family:
Discover the Rich Apple Ecosystem of the Mac, iPhone, iPad, and Apple TV

Jeff Carlson and Dan Moren

Peachpit Press
www.peachpit.com

To report errors, please send a note to errata@peachpit.com
Peachpit Press is a division of Pearson Education

Editors: Clifford Colby and Scout Festa
Production editor: David Van Ness
Copyeditor: Scout Festa
Compositors: Jeff Carlson and Danielle Foster
Indexer: Valerie Haynes Perry
Cover Design: Aren Straiger
Interior Design: Mimi Heft

Notice of Rights

Notice of Liability

Trademarks

ISBN 13:   978-0-134-03624-3
ISBN 10:   0-134-03624-7

9 8 7 6 5 4 3 2 1
Printed and bound in the United States of America

To Kimberly and Ellie, who can never receive too many dedications.
—Jeff

To my parents, Harold and Sally, for their unfailing encouragement and a lifelong love of books.
—Dan

Acknowledgments

Our sincere thanks go out to the following people, who made it possible for us to produce this book:

Cliff Colby, for pushing the project into existence at Peachpit Press and moving the publishing machinery as needed to allow us to do the book

Scout Festa for her keen copyediting and proofing skills

Valerie Haynes Perry for writing the index (an underappreciated art)

David Van Ness for coordinating the book's production

Danielle Foster for her layout assistance

Mimi Heft for designing an excellent book and template design

Heidi Blondin, Bert Hopkins, Logan Blondin, and Eliana Carlson for being fantastic models

Everyone involved in printing, binding, and shipping the print book around the world

Contents

Introduction

In the early days of personal computing, using a computer was simple.

Typically you had only one computer. All you had to do was learn how to operate that computer and the software you put on it, and you'd be set.

Well, come to think of it, that was often pretty darn complicated. You had to know which commands to type, which components to install, and more often than not, have a little programming experience under your belt.

And then things started getting easier, at least from the point of view of the people buying and using computers. The Macintosh was introduced as the "computer for the rest of us," with its graphical user interface that describes what we still see today (on Windows PCs, too): mouse pointers, icons, folders and files, clicking-and-dragging.

The Mac made computers friendly without sacrificing processing power, and then the iPhone and iPad made things easier still: People don't have to worry about underlying file systems or obscure network protocols. Children immediately understand how to use the touch interface of iOS.

Today, with an array of devices—computers, phones, tablets, fitness sensors, and wearables such as the upcoming Apple Watch—"computing" has merged into our everyday activities. When you look up driving directions on your iPhone, you're tapping into a powerful computer connected to a worldwide wireless network. We don't think of it as "working with a computer," because it is, from our point of view, a simple task.

And yet, computing is still difficult.

The products are all designed to work together—look at Handoff or AirDrop for passing documents among devices, or iCloud for syncing data—but how? Apple introduced Family Sharing in iOS 8 and OS X Yosemite to finally help families and friends centrally manage apps and media, but the feature carries a few significant limitations (for example, a user can join a family group only twice per year).

This book is your guide through the Apple ecosystem (or "geekosystem," as one friend described it), revealing the best ways to connect these devices.

Notes About This Book

We're making a few assumptions about you, dear reader, to make sure we're all on the same page:

- You have more than one Apple device, and probably more than one person using those devices.

- You know the basics of using Apple's products. We don't expect you to be an expert, but as long as you can get around easily, you're good.

- Most likely, you're the one who has volunteered (or has been tasked) as the go-to person expected to understand all this and set it up for everyone else. In Apple's parlance, that makes you the *Family Organizer* (we'll go into more detail in Chapter 1). If you're not, this book is still helpful in making Apple's ecosystem work—for example, if you're not using the Family Sharing feature, or you know that one day you may find yourself the Family Organizer.

- You and the members of your Apple family—which can be a mix of blood relatives and friends—are running OS X Yosemite (version 10.10) on Macs and iOS 8 on any iPhone, iPad, or iPod touch devices.

As you read, you'll run into examples where we've adopted general terms or phrases to avoid getting distracted by details. For example, we may refer to the "computer" or the "desktop" as shorthand for any traditional computer that isn't an iPad or iPhone.

The same general rule applies to iPad and iPhone models. For example, the iPad mini, despite its size, is still a fully functional iPad, so when we refer to "iPad" in general it applies to the iPad mini as well as to the larger, flagship model. Similarly, we don't always refer to specific models.

We also frequently refer to just the iPhone even though the information applies equally well to the iPod touch. We're not being lazy, for two reasons: If we had to always type "iPhone, iPad, and iPod touch," we'd go quickly insane. Also, as we write this, the latest iPod touch Apple sells is the fifth-generation model, which was originally released in 2012. We suspect that unless Apple has something up its sleeve, the iPod touch as we know it will soon disappear.

When directing you to specific areas within iOS and OS X, we use a short-hand for locating them. For example, to access the preferences for the

Camera app, we'll point you to **Settings > Photos & Camera**. That translates to "open the Settings app and tap the Photos & Camera button" (1).

On the Mac, settings are called preference panes and found in System Preferences. So when we ask you to open the iCloud preference pane, it means "open System Preferences and click the iCloud icon" (2).

1 Photos & Camera settings on the iPad

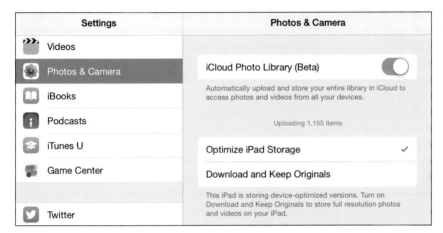

2 Accessing the iCloud preference pane on OS X

CHAPTER 1

Welcome to the Apple Family

One of the most common frustrations of working with a multitude of Apple devices is how separated they can be. We switch between devices throughout any given day—iPhone when out and about, Mac while working or studying, iPad to catch up on news and reading at night, just to name a few situations—but until recently, each device existed mostly in its own little bubble. A few tendrils enabled limited communication, such as sharing calendars via iCloud, but using multiple devices always felt like a juggling act. Now, iOS 8 and OS X Yosemite bring those disparate devices closer together. For example, Apple's Continuity features, such as Handoff for moving documents quickly between devices, reduce the friction of juggling documents and email messages.

However, it's not all about your own mini arsenal of glass and aluminum products. The Apple unification starts with Family Sharing, a feature that finally makes it easy to share media like music and videos among the devices owned by other people you include in a family group.

The Basics of Family Sharing

First off, let's define *family* in this context. For Family Sharing, Apple envisions a traditional nuclear family, with parents, children, siblings, and so forth, either living in the same household or close enough that the products are easily at hand. Of course, in the real world a family can encompass lots of other variations: close friends, cousins, grandparents who live over the river and through the woods....

So, a "family" for our purposes is any combination of those, with the practical limitation being that a Family can include up to *six* people. (Why just six? Our guess is that six is a reasonable compromise between Apple and the media companies who are traditionally paranoid about people misappropriating content.) Each family member must have their own free Apple ID, which is what they created when setting up their Apple product. If someone does not have an Apple ID, go to appleid.apple.com and click Create an Apple ID. A person can be a member of only one family at a time.

▶ **NOTE** The process of setting up an Apple ID for a child age 13 or under is different than normal. See "Create an Apple ID for a Child," and, if necessary, "Convert an Existing Apple ID to a Child ID," later in this chapter.

▶ **NOTE** An account can set up or join a Family group only twice a year.

Family Sharing works under iOS 8 and OS X Yosemite. Compatible devices include:

- iPhone 4s, iPhone 5, iPhone 5s, iPhone 6, iPhone 6 Plus
- iPod touch (5th generation) and later
- iMac (Mid 2007 or newer)
- MacBook Air (Late 2008 or newer)
- MacBook (Late 2008 Aluminum, or Early 2009 or newer)
- Mac mini (Early 2009 or newer)
- MacBook Pro (Mid/Late 2007 or newer)
- Mac Pro (Early 2008 or newer)
- Xserve (Early 2009)

Family Sharing isn't turned on by default. If you manage only your own devices, feel free to skip to the next chapter.

Set Up the Family Organizer

One person in the Family Sharing family needs to be the Family Organizer, who is responsible for all purchases of music, movies, TV shows, and apps. We're guessing that's you—congratulations! (If it's not you, make sure the person who will assume the job has the following instructions.)

You can configure your Apple ID to be the Family Organizer on an iOS device or on a Mac. Here are the steps for both environments.

iOS 8

To set up Family Sharing on an iOS device, do the following:

1. Go to Settings > iCloud.

2. Tap Set Up Family Sharing (1.1).

1.1 iCloud settings

3. Tap Get Started.

4. Make sure you're signed in to the personal account that will be the Family Organizer, and then tap Continue. If you're not, tap the link "Not (name of person) or want to use a different ID?" and enter another Apple ID and password you wish to use. Tap Continue.

5. On the Share Purchases screen, tap Continue after you understand that your Apple ID will be shared among the other devices you set up, and that everyone will be able to view and download your purchased media.

Alternately, if that Apple ID doesn't have payment information on record, you may have to enter your Apple ID and password again. Do so and tap Next.

Since the Organizer needs a credit card account, tap Go to Settings, which takes you to the iTunes & App Store settings. Sign in using your Apple ID, then tap the Apple ID field again and tap View Apple ID.

On the Account Settings screen, tap Payment Information, enter your credit card number and billing information, and tap Done.

6. At the Payment Method screen, Apple really wants you to understand that anyone in your family can potentially bleed your bank account dry if you proceed. Don't worry, we'll set up measures to protect against that, so go ahead and tap Continue.

7. On the next screen, you can share your device's location with other members of the family. Tap Share Your Location to enable this, or Not Now to skip it until later. Your Apple ID is now set up as the Family Organizer.

OS X Yosemite

If you're setting up Family Sharing on a Mac, follow these steps:

1. Go to System Preferences > iCloud.

2. Click Set Up Family (1.2).

3. Click Continue.

1.2 iCloud settings in OS X Yosemite

4. When asked if you'd like to be the Family Organizer, make sure you're signed in to the Apple ID you want to use and click Continue.

5. Confirm the Apple ID and password. Click Continue.

   If your account does not have payment information associated with it, you'll need to set that up in iTunes before you can continue:

   Launch iTunes and choose Store > Sign In.

   In the Edit Payment Information screen, type your credit card and billing details and click Done (1.3). Then go back to the iCloud preference pane and repeat steps 1 through 4.

1.3 Enter your credit card information in iTunes.

6. Read the iTunes and Family Sharing terms and conditions and click Agree.

7. Your Apple ID is now set up as the Family Organizer. Click Done to dismiss the family list.

   ▶ **NOTE** Once an Apple ID is set up in Family Sharing, any device that uses the ID is automatically configured. For example, you wouldn't need to do anything extra for an iPad you own that uses the same Apple ID as the iPhone or Mac you set up.

Congratulations, you've just started a(n Apple) Family!

Invite Family Members

As the Family Organizer, it's up to you to invite other people to join your virtual family—they can't add themselves. The process is nearly identical on iOS and OS X, so we're going to combine the steps here:

1. Go to the iCloud settings on your iOS device or Mac and tap the Family button (iOS) or click the Manage Family button (OS X).

2. On the Family screen, tap or click Add Family Member.

3. Type the name (if the person is already in your list of contacts) or email address of the person you want to add (1.4). Tap Next or click Continue.

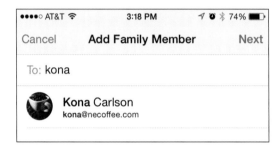

4. You may be asked to verify your credit card's security number. After that, choose between two options:

   • **Ask to Enter Password:** If the person is there with you, he or she can use your device to enter their Apple ID password and click or tap Continue.

   • **Send an Invitation:** An invitation should appear momentarily on the family member's device. Swipe the notification on the lock screen (if the device is asleep), or tap the notification that appears to view the invitation in the iCloud settings. An email message is also sent.

   The recipient can accept or decline the invitation. If it didn't go through for whatever reason, you can tap or click their name and resend it.

   If you change your mind suddenly, and they haven't yet replied, you can rescind the invitation by selecting their name and either tapping Remove (iOS) or clicking the minus-sign (–) button (OS X).

5. The recipient is asked to confirm they want to join the Family, and reminded that other family members will be able to view their purchased media.

6. Lastly, the recipient can choose to share their location with the rest of the family.

Just like that, your family is growing! Repeat for any other adult you wish to add; they appear in your Family Members list (1.5).

1.5 A growing Family

Create an Apple ID for a Child

As a consequence of us owning and reviewing several generations of Apple equipment over the years, there's seemingly no end to old hardware that can be passed down to kids, nieces, and nephews. In the past, though, that meant setting up, say, an iPad with our own Apple IDs in order to manage apps and media purchases.

Family Sharing finally lets children have their own accounts, managed by the Family Organizer. Namely, kids can order an app or media, but the transaction isn't complete until you approve it.

▶ **NOTE** To create a child account, you need a *credit card*, not a debit card, on file for your account. The signup process won't proceed until a credit card is on file. Go to the iTunes & App Store settings on iOS, or open iTunes on your Mac and choose Store > View Account, to enter your credit card information.

The Family Sharing setup includes an option to create a new Apple ID for children. If you've already set up a regular Apple ID for a child prior to iOS 8, we'll discuss how to convert it shortly.

The process of entering the child's information differs by platform—on iOS, it's a series of screens; on the Mac, it's all in one dialog.

iOS 8

1. Go to the iCloud settings on an iOS device or a Mac and tap Family.

2. Look at the very bottom of the screen and tap the link that says "Create an Apple ID for a child" (1.6). Tap Next on the following screen.

1.6 The option to create a child account is nestled at the bottom of thescreen.

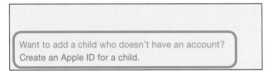

3. Start by entering the child's birthdate and tap Next.

4. Agree to the Parent Privacy Disclosure. Then enter the security code for your credit card to verify that you are the parent or legal guardian.

5. Enter the child's first and last names and tap Next.

6. Type the Apple ID you'd like to use and tap Next (1.7). If the ID already exists, you're asked to choose a new one.

1.7 Choose a unique address for the child.

7. Choose a password that you and the child will both remember. Enter it in the Password and Verify fields and tap Next.

8. Set up security questions by tapping the Question field, choosing a question, entering an answer, and tapping Next to continue. Apple asks for three questions. Note that these are questions for you, not the child.

9. On the next screen, keep Ask To Buy enabled and tap Next.

10. Tap Share Location to enable location sharing.

11. Agree to the Apple and iTunes terms and conditions.

OS X Yosemite

1. Go to the iCloud settings on a Mac and click Manage Family.

   Click the Add (+) button and then select the option labeled "Create an Apple ID for a child who doesn't have an account." Click Continue.

2. Enter the child's birthdate.

3. Type the Apple ID you'd like to use. If the ID already exists, you'll be asked to choose a new one after you click Continue.

4. Enter the child's first and last names.

5. Choose a password that you and the child will both remember. Enter it in the Password and Verify fields (1.8).

1.8 Creating a child account in OS X Yosemite

6. Click Continue, and then click OK to confirm you want to create the ID.

7. Enter the security code for your credit card to verify that you are the child's legal parent or guardian and click Agree to abide by the Parent Privacy Disclosure.

8. Set up three security questions by choosing from the pop-up menus and entering answers. Note that these are questions for you, not the child. Click Continue.

9. Agree to the terms and conditions for iCloud, Game Center, and iTunes.

10. Click Done to exit the Manage Family dialog.

Convert an Existing Apple ID to a Child ID

Before Family Sharing, you may have created a regular Apple ID to use with a child's device or for Game Center. You don't need to abandon it (and any media you've accumulated using it) in order to toggle the Ask To Pay option. However, the workaround is a little…sketchy.

1. Sign in using the Apple ID you want to convert at appleid.apple.com.

2. Click Manage your Apple ID.

3. Enter your ID and password.

4. Click the Password and Security option. (If the account has two-step verification enabled, click the Name, ID, and Email Addresses option.)

5. Under Select Your Birth Date, set the date as **January 1, 2001** (1.9).

6. Click Save. iCloud now recognizes your account as belonging to a teen.

7. Go to one of your Family Organizer devices, open the iCloud settings, and tap the name of the new child account. Or, on a Mac, go to the iCloud preference pane, click Manage Family, select the child account, and enable the Ask To Buy option; click Done.

1.9 2001: An Apple ID odyssey

▶ **NOTE** This approach does seem like a hack, so we wouldn't be surprised if Apple either blocks this route or institutes a formal method of converting an pre-Family Sharing adult Apple ID to a child one.

Edit a Shared Family

As Family Organizer, you can remove members, transfer child accounts, or disband the Family group altogether. In the iCloud settings, tap the name of the Family (iOS) or click the Manage Family button (OS X) and do the following:

- To remove an adult family member under iOS, tap their name and then tap the Remove button. On a Mac, click the minus-sign (–) under the family list and then click Remove.

- Children under 13 cannot be removed from a Family, but they can be transferred to a new Family. Ask the Family Organizer of the new Family to extend an invitation to the child's Apple ID, and then accept the invite on the child's device.

- To disband a Shared Family, which breaks the link to all members, select your Apple ID and tap Stop Family Sharing (iOS) or click the minus-sign (–) button (OS X) (1.10, on the next page). Any pending Ask to Buy requests are cancelled. (Ask to Buy is covered in the next chapter.)

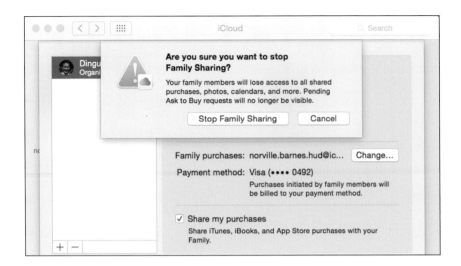

> ▶ **NOTE** A Family can't be disbanded if there are child IDs in it. They must be transferred to another Family first. For more information, see Apple's documentation: http://support.apple.com/kb/HT201081.

After leaving or disbanding a Family, your shared media doesn't vanish in a virtual puff of smoke, but it won't be usable: you'll need to purchase items to continue using them, or remove them from a device to regain storage space. Shared photos, calendars, and reminders do go away. And if you downloaded a shared app and made in-app purchases, you'll need to buy the app yourself to reactivate the in-app purchases.

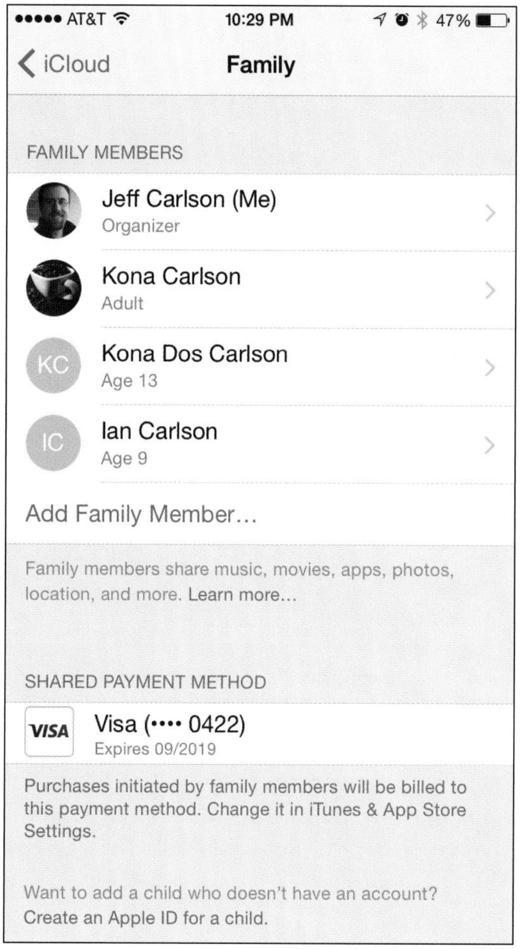

1.11 The Family

CHAPTER 2

Share Apps and Media

A Family Sharing group is great for sharing calendars and keeping track of other members' locations (which we cover elsewhere in the book), but to us the real advantage is being able to share apps and media.

For example, have you ever wanted to listen to an album and realized it's on your partner's computer or iOS device? Before our music was digitized, you'd borrow or burn a CD. Family Sharing sets up an architecture that dramatically simplifies the process and puts the emphasis back on *sharing*—not just as the transportation of bits between devices, but as the exchange and discovery of new good music and other media.

The same applies to ebooks, movies, TV shows, and apps you've purchased. And don't forget photos, now that we capture so many pictures with iPhones.

Of course, Family Sharing isn't the only way to share between devices and people. We cover plenty of non-Family options, too.

Purchase Media

Apple runs the three main methods of acquiring media for your Mac or iOS device: the iTunes Store, the App Store, and the Mac App Store. Of those, the App Store is the exclusive method of purchasing iOS apps. (Confusingly, you can also purchase iOS apps from the iTunes Store on a Mac.) Apple's control over the buying experience enables you to do things like automatically install apps on every device, restrict which items are purchased by other members of the Family group, and require youngsters to get your permission before buying something.

Auto-Install on Your Other Devices

Most iOS apps run on both the iPhone (and iPod touch) and iPad, so if you own multiple devices, you can purchase an app in one place and find it installed on the others. The same applies to music and ebooks in iBooks; since videos require so much storage, they aren't included in this feature on iOS. To set this up, go to Settings > iTunes & App Store and turn on Automatic Downloads for Music, Apps, or Books (2.1).

▶ **NOTE** Automatic installation works only on devices that are signed in with the same Apple ID. You can't auto-install apps on a device with someone else's ID, even if it's a member of your Family group.

2.1 Automatic Download settings in iTunes on iOS

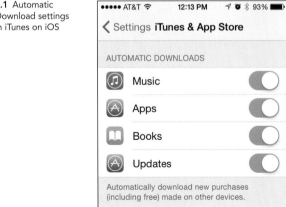

On the Mac, the options are a little different. In iTunes, choose iTunes > Preferences and click the Store button at the top of the dialog (2.2). Here you can opt to automatically download music and apps, as well as movies and TV shows. In this case, since a Mac has more storage and a better Internet connection, video is allowed.

2.2 Automatic Download settings in iTunes on OS X

What you don't see in iTunes, however, is an option for books. So, to auto-install ebooks you've purchased, open the iBooks application, choose iBooks > Preferences, click the Store button, and enable Download New Purchases Automatically (2.3).

▶ **TIP** On iOS devices, the iTunes & App Store settings include the Use Cellular Data option, which automatically downloads media and app updates without requiring a Wi-Fi connection. This feature is convenient, but it does count against your monthly usage allotment, so turn the option off if you're concerned you might incur overage charges from your cellular provider.

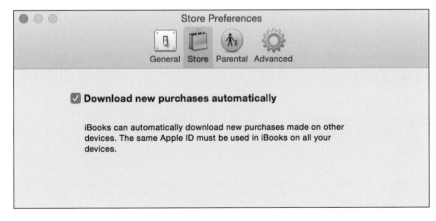

2.3 Automatic book downloads settings in iBooks on OS X

Ask to Buy

Under Family Sharing, all members of the group make media or app purchases that are charged to the same credit card. That's great for tracking expenses, but does open a door through which money flies out at an alarming rate (either purposefully or accidentally; young kids may not understand how much money could be eaten up by games' in-app purchases).

The Ask to Buy feature ensures that every potential purchase is approved by the Family Organizer or someone set up to also grant approval. Note that Ask to Buy appears only for accounts designated 13 years of age or younger. Here's how it works.

To set up Ask to Buy, do the following:

1. Go to Settings > iCloud on the iOS device belonging to the Family Organizer, or open the iCloud preference pane on a Mac signed in to the organizer's Apple ID.

2. Tap the Family button (iOS) or click Manage Family (OS X).

3. Select the child family member you want to edit.

4. Tap or click the Ask to Buy button to enable it (2.4). On the Mac, click Done.

▶ **NOTE** The first time you set up Ask to Buy, you need to sign the child in to the App Store and iTunes Store apps using his or her account and password, and you may be asked to provide the security code of the organizer's credit card.

2.4 Setting up Ask to Buy for a child account

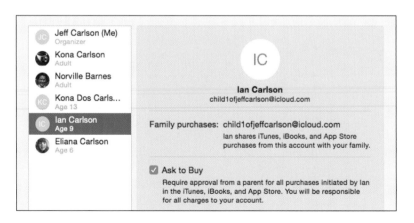

When the child wants to purchase something, the process works like this:

1. The child finds something in the App Store, the iTunes Store, or the iBooks Store and taps the price button (which becomes a Buy button).

2. In the Ask Permission dialog that appears, tap Ask (2.5).

3. On the organizer's devices, a notification about the purchase shows up. On the Mac, click the Details button, or click Not Now to dismiss the notification. On an iOS device, slide the notification to review the request.

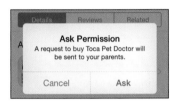 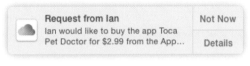

2.5 Making a purchase on an iOS device (left) and the notification that appears on the Family Organizer's Mac (right)

4. Tap or click Approve or Decline (2.6). If you approved the purchase, the item is installed.

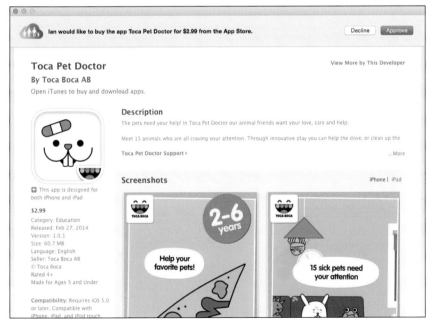

2.6 The Ask to Buy approval dialog on OS X

Set Up an Adult as a Parent/Guardian

To share the load of approving purchases, you can set up another adult member of your Family group as a Parent/Guardian. Open the iCloud settings on a Mac or iOS device, view your group, and select the person you want to anoint as being responsible. Enable the Parent/Guardian option (2.7).

▶ **NOTE** It's also possible to disable all purchases on the device—this is the mechanism you need to use if you don't have Family Sharing enabled. See "Set Up Restrictions," later in this chapter.

2.7 Granting an adult Family group member the ability to approve Ask to Buy requests

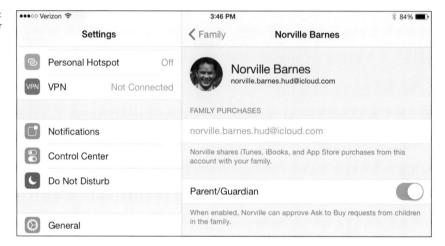

Set Up a Monthly Allowance

Apple offers another way to help you manage purchases, which it calls an iTunes Allowance. Instead of pulling funds from the Family Sharing credit card for each purchase, an amount you choose from $10 to $50 is debited from your account and made available to someone with an Apple ID. That gives purchasing flexibility to someone without a credit card, like a child. iTunes Allowance is also an option if you choose not to sign up with Family Sharing. Here's how to set it up:

1. In iTunes on your computer, choose Store > View Account and sign in to your iTunes account.

2. On the Account Information screen, scroll down to the Settings area and locate the Allowances item. Click Set Up an Allowance.

3. Fill in the name of the person getting the allowance, choose an amount to be paid monthly, and decide whether to send the first installment now or wait until the first of next month (2.8).

2.8 Creating an iTunes Allowance

4. Enter the Apple ID of the recipient (and again to verify the address).

5. Optionally enter a message and click Continue.

6. Enter your Apple ID and password and click Set Up.

7. On the Confirm Your Purchase screen, click Buy. The recipient's account is credited the amount you chose.

▶ **NOTE** You can suspend or remove the allowance by signing back in to iTunes and clicking the Manage button for Allowances.

Share Purchased Apps and Media

At the start of this chapter we dangled the possibility of sharing media between Family Sharing members' devices, so how does it work? Although you might expect everyone's media would simply appear on other devices, instead you must download the content via the respective store apps.

On an iOS device, do the following:

1. Open the App Store (for sharing apps), the iTunes Store (music, movies, or TV shows), or the iBooks (ebooks) app.

2. Access the Purchased screen: On the iPad, it's a button at the bottom of the app. On the iPhone and iPod touch, first tap the Updates button in the App Store or the More button in the iTunes Store and then choose Purchased (2.9). In the iBooks app, the Purchased button appears at the bottom of the screen on all devices.

2.9 Accessing media purchased by other Family Sharing members on iOS

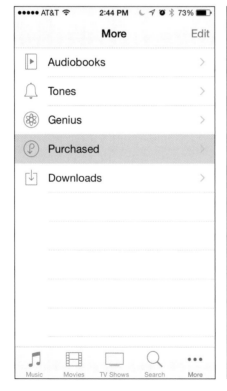
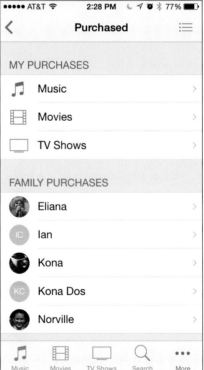

3. On the iPhone and iPod touch, tap the name of the Family member whose media or app you want to download.

   On the iPad, by default you're shown the purchases for your own account. To view other members' items, tap the My Purchases button (2.10) and choose the Family member you want to copy from.

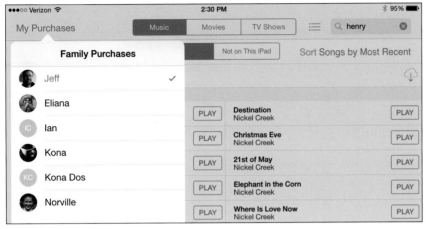

2.10 Accessing purchases on the iPad

4. Locate the item you want. For media, first tap the type (Music, Movies, or TV Shows) and then narrow your choice to a specific album, track, movie, or TV episode.

   It's usually helpful to tap the Not on This iPad/iPhone/iPod button to narrow the field and ignore items already on the device.

5. To download an app, tap the Free button, which becomes an Install App button (2.11); tap again to add the app to the device.

   To download music, movies, TV shows, or books, tap the iCloud download button next to the item you want (2.12).

2.11 Downloading purchased music

2.12 Downloading purchased apps

▶ **TIP** On the iPhone and iPod touch, when faced with someone's app library that includes dozens or hundreds of items, swipe down to reveal a Search field that lets you find what you're looking for just within the purchases list. On the iPad, the Search field is located above the list. For media, tap the alphabet navigation at left.

▶ **TIP** In the iTunes app on the iPad, viewing the list of music from one of the Family group members can be initially misleading: The middle of the screen reads "[Family member] does not have any music available to you," even though that's untrue. Tap the alphabetical navigation at left to view artists. We hope this is just a bug that's fixed by the time you read this.

▶ **NOTE** If you prefer to read ebooks purchased from Amazon using its Kindle app, you *may* be able to lend a book to someone. A title can be loaned only once, the other person can have it for only 14 days, and you can't read the book during that time. Also, not all books are enabled for lending. Check the book's product page at Amazon.com: In the Product Details section, look for the Lending line to see if it's even possible.

Home Sharing

So far, we've focused on how to share apps and media among Family Sharing groups, but that's not the only way to do it. Home Sharing enables devices on the same network to stream media from iTunes on a Mac or Windows computer, as well as copy media among devices. It can also be used alongside Family Sharing; for example, enabling you to watch a movie stored on a Mac in another room instead of streaming it from the Internet (and possibly counting against a bandwidth cap imposed by your Internet provider).

Home Sharing requires you to set up all devices with one Apple ID. To enable it on a Mac, open iTunes and choose File > Home Sharing > Turn On Home Sharing. Enter your Apple ID and password and click the Turn On Home Sharing button.

On an iOS device, open Settings and select either the Music or Videos settings. Under Home Sharing, enter the same Apple ID and password as you did on the Mac (2.13) and tap Done or the Return key.

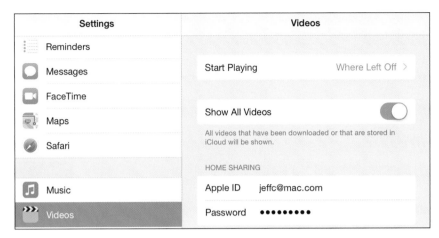

2.13 Turning on Home Sharing

Settings	Videos
Reminders	
Messages	Start Playing Where Left Off >
FaceTime	
Maps	Show All Videos
Safari	All videos that have been downloaded or that are stored in iCloud will be shown.
	HOME SHARING
Music	Apple ID jeffc@mac.com
Videos	Password ••••••••

Share Media via Home Sharing

With Home Sharing set up, you can play music or videos as if they were on the device, but without needing to copy the files.

On an iOS device, do the following:

1. Open the Videos app and tap the new Shared category. Or, in the Music app, tap the More button and then tap Shared.

2. Tap the name of the computer you wish to connect to. After a few seconds, the library on the computer to which you're connected appears; its name is listed at the top of the screen to identify which library you're browsing (2.14).

3. Browse the library and tap the item you want to watch or listen to.

2.14 Browsing a shared library on the iPad

To return to the device's library, go back to the Shared category and select the device's name at the top of the list.

To share media between computers using iTunes, click the Home Sharing icon at the left of the toolbar and choose a shared library (2.15).

2.15 The Home Sharing icon and menu

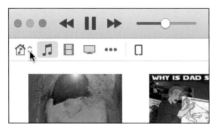 

Import Media via Home Sharing

Home Sharing also enables you to copy media between computers, either manually or automatically. This ability is great if you have a spare Mac being used as a media server on your network and you want to make sure that master library includes items you've purchased on your computer. For example, let's say you're headed out of town and you want to copy a few movies you own onto your MacBook Pro. If you purchased them from Apple, you could just stream them over the Internet, but hotel connections are notoriously ill-equipped for streaming media. Use Home Sharing to copy the video files directly.

1. In iTunes, connect to the other computer on your network that has the files you want, as described previously.

2. Locate the media you want to add to your library; it may be helpful to choose Items Not in My Library from the Show pop-up menu (2.16).

3. Click the Import button to copy the file(s).

2.16 Importing media via Home Sharing in iTunes

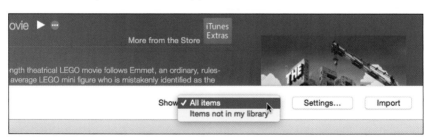

To automatically import new items (such as from your computer to your media server Mac), click the Settings button and select the categories to be copied. Click OK to apply the setting.

This feature applies only to new media added after you enable the auto import. To bring over items already in the library, import them manually.

iTunes Match

You'd think two methods of sharing music would be enough, but no, Apple offers a third: iTunes Match, a paid service that costs $24.99 a year. In this case, the focus is less on sharing music with other people and more on making your music library available on any device you own without needing to synchronize anything. It's also good for dealing with limited storage: You don't need to carry all the files in your entire music library on your iPhone, for example, but you can stream or download any of it as needed.

When you subscribe, iTunes compares your music library to the entire iTunes catalog. Anything not in the catalog is uploaded to iCloud for you to stream or download. iTunes Match also offers iTunes Radio without ads.

To enable iTunes Match, go to iTunes and choose Store > Turn On iTunes Match. On an iOS device, go to Settings > iTunes & App Store and tap Subscribe to iTunes Match. Or, if you've already subscribed and the device's primary iCloud account is the same as the one you signed up with, simply turn on the iTunes Match switch.

Music stored in the cloud appears in the Music app or in iTunes with an iCloud icon. Tap or click a song or album title to stream the music without storing it on your device, or tap or click the iCloud icon to download the track(s).

▶ **TIP** An added benefit of iTunes Match is the ability to re-download higher quality versions of songs than what you have. Music ripped from your CDs years ago may have been encoded at a lower rate. After iTunes Match is finished matching your library, delete the lower-quality tracks (making sure to *not* remove them from iCloud when prompted), and then re-download them. That also applies to tracks in your library that still have leftover DRM (digital rights management); in most cases, the version you download will be DRM-free.

Movie Rentals

Although we've covered how to share videos among devices using Family Sharing and Home Sharing, there's one area that requires further discussion: movie rentals. We love the ability to rent nearly any new release—and increasingly, movies that are available via iTunes before or simultaneous with their theatrical releases—without leaving the house. However, no doubt due to the machinations of movie studios, rentals are encumbered by a lot of rules and limitations.

There are two essential ground rules:

- After you rent a movie, you must watch it within 30 days.

- However, once you start watching the movie, it's available for only 24 hours, after which it's automatically deleted.

A movie can be rented on any device—Mac, iPad, iPhone, iPod touch, and the Apple TV—but you should consider how you plan to watch the flick before choose where to rent.

- If you plan to watch the movie on a particular device, such as on an iPad, go ahead and rent it there.

- If you want to watch a movie on a Mac *or* an iOS device, rent it in iTunes on the Mac or on a Windows PC. A rental can be transferred between iTunes and an iOS device, but it can't live in both places; iTunes tracks where the movie is stored back at Apple headquarters to prevent people from making copies. Unfortunately, if you rent a movie on an iOS device, it cannot be moved to iTunes on a computer.

- If you want to watch a movie on an Apple TV, and only there, rent it on the Apple TV. Rentals initiated on the Apple TV are locked to it.

- If you want to watch a movie on an iOS device or an Apple TV, rent it on the iOS device. You can stream the movie from the device to the Apple TV using AirPlay (see the next section about the Apple TV).

- For the most flexibility to watch a rental on any device, rent it in iTunes on a computer. That gives you the option of watching the movie on the computer, transferring the rental to an iOS device, or streaming to an Apple TV from the computer.

► **NOTE** To encourage sales, Apple usually makes new releases available for rent several weeks after their initial appearance in the store.

To rent a movie, follow these steps:

1. Locate the movie in the iTunes Store (in iTunes on a Mac or PC), the iTunes app (on iOS), or the Movies category (Apple TV).

2. Tap, click, or select the Rent button (2.17), which turns into a Rent Movie (or Rent HD Movie) button.

3. Select that button; you're asked to enter your Apple ID and password to begin downloading the film. If you rented on the Apple TV, you can start watching the movie after a few minutes.

► **NOTE** Rentals work the same as purchases for Family Sharing groups: If a child with Ask to Buy enabled wants to rent a movie, the request must be approved by the Family Organizer or a member designated as a Parent/Guardian.

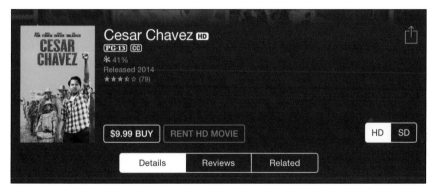

2.17 Renting a movie on the iPad

Transfer a Rental from iTunes

The ability to transfer a rental to an iOS device is a holdover from the pre-iCloud days when the only way to add media to an iPhone, iPad, or iPod touch was to sync it through iTunes. To move a rental between devices still requires this route, because a rental can exist on only one device at a time. And remember, this works only with rentals you've downloaded in iTunes on a computer; you can't transfer a movie rented on an iOS device to iTunes.

1. Connect the device to the computer via the sync cable. (Wi-Fi syncing also works if you've set it up, but doing it via cable is faster.)

2. In iTunes, select the device from the toolbar and click the Movies setting in the sidebar.

3. In the Rented Movies section, click the Move button for the rental you wish to transfer (2.18).

4. Click the Apply button at the bottom of the window to initiate the transfer. iTunes needs to check in with the Apple mothership to make the move happen, so you need an Internet connection when you attempt the move.

2.18 Moving a rental from iTunes to an iPad

After several minutes, the movie appears in the Videos app of the device under a new Rentals category.

Thirty days sounds like a long time, but believe us from experience, it can go by quickly if you don't intend to watch the movie right away. iTunes or the Videos app will notify you within a few days of the end of rental period. You can also go to the Rentals screen of the Videos app or iTunes to see how many days are left before it expires.

Apple TV

Once considered a "hobby" by Apple, the Apple TV is now a hugely successful business by itself and a key extension of the Apple ecosystem. You can stream content from several providers, such as Netflix; order and watch movies, TV shows, and music from the iTunes Store; and stream video and audio (and games!) from Macs or iOS devices using AirPlay.

▶ **TIP** Assuming you have an iOS device, we recommend that you download Apple's Remote app. With it, you can control the Apple TV—the screen acts like a trackpad—but more convenient is the ability to use the iOS keyboard when you need to type information instead of relying on the Apple TV's key layout, which is run by the physical remote.

Play Media Using Family Sharing

First up, you'll need to set up the Apple TV for Family Sharing, if you haven't already done so. Go to Settings > iCloud and enter your Apple ID. The unit recognizes other members in your Family group. You can watch movies and TV shows using Family Sharing; listening to music is not supported, alas.

To play media purchased by other members, do the following:

1. Select the Movies button, and press the center Select button on the Apple remote.

2. Select Shared Movies, and select the Family member whose media you want to view (2.19).

2.19 Accessing Family members' shared movies on the Apple TV

3. Select the movie you want to view, and press the Select button.

4. On the movie's title screen, select Play (2.20). If the movie offers iTunes Extras, you need to select the Play button on the next screen (or you can enjoy the extras). The movie streams from Apple's servers.

2.20 Family Sharing on the Apple TV is awesome.

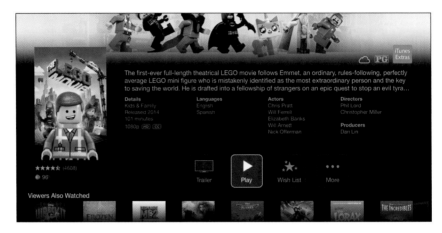

Play Media Using Home Sharing

As with Home Sharing on personal devices, the feature on the Apple TV lets you stream content from iTunes running Macs or Windows PCs on your network.

1. On the main Apple TV screen, select the Computers category (2.21).

2.21 Home Sharing via the Computers category

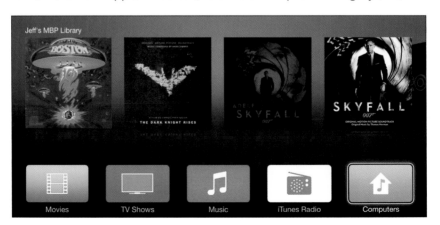

2. Choose a computer you've set up to share content from the Computers list on the next screen.

3. Navigate to the music, movie, TV show, home video (any video not purchased from iTunes), or podcast. Select the item to play it.

Play Media via AirPlay

So far, the options for playing media on an Apple TV have all been pretty structured. What if you want to switch from watching a movie on your iPad to the Apple TV? Or play a quick YouTube clip or a video you shot with your iPhone on the big screen, where others can see it? Or continue listening to an album in the Music app through the speakers connected to your TV? AirPlay is the answer. Make sure AirPlay is enabled in Settings > AirPlay on the Apple TV, and then do the following:

1. On your iOS device, swipe up from the bottom to open Control Center.

2. Tap the AirPlay button and choose the Apple TV (2.22). The playback buttons on the device control the movie, as does the Apple TV's remote.

2.22 AirPlay options in Control Center

In some cases, the AirPlay icon may appear at the bottom of a video you're playing, letting you play just that item without switching all playback to the Apple TV, as in the steps above.

In iTunes, click the AirPlay button next to the playback controls (at the top of the window, or in the floating controls that appear when a movie is playing) and choose the Apple TV as the destination (2.23).

▶ **TIP** The Apple TV isn't a game console, per se, but some developers have included AirPlay functionality into games so that the iOS device acts as a controller or accessory. As with sharing media, open Control Center and choose the Apple TV as the AirPlay destination.

2.23 AirPlay options in iTunes

Photos

It's difficult to underestimate the impact photography has had on our lives. What was once a discipline that required hardware and training is now open to anyone with an iOS device (mostly iPhones), which means more people are capturing more photos than ever. But the ability to shoot good photos—thanks in part to the camera technology in the iPhone and iPad— is only part of the story. Being able to *shoot and share* photos immediately has had a more profound effect. Photos don't have to be locked into their camera anymore; a shot taken with an iPhone can be shared with friends, family members, and the entire world within minutes.

iCloud Photo Library

Apple's approach to sharing photos relies on iCloud. The new iCloud Photo Library, introduced in iOS 8 and OS X Yosemite, uploads your photos to iCloud and, by default, stores optimized versions on the device to reduce the amount of storage consumed. To turn on iCloud Photo Library, go to Settings > iCloud > Photos and enable the iCloud Photo Library switch (2.24).

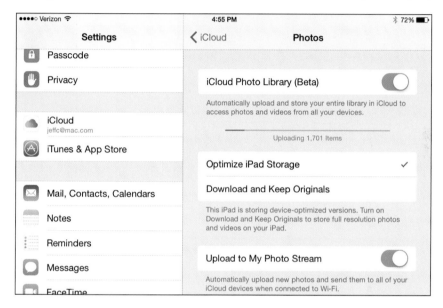

2.24 Activating iCloud Photo Library

▶ **NOTE** As we write this, iCloud Photo Library is still officially a beta, which means the software isn't final enough to be considered a full release, but Apple is hoping people will report problems to be fixed. If you'd prefer to wait for the bugs to get worked out, don't turn it on. You'll use the iOS 7-style approach, which stores all photos on your device and gives you the option of turning on iCloud Photo Stream to copy photos to iCloud. The ability to create albums specifically for iCloud Photo Sharing, described shortly, is still available.

▶ **TIP** If you'd prefer to store the original versions of your photos instead of the optimized versions on your device, go to Settings > iCloud > Photos and select Download and Keep Originals. Remember, even if you leave Optimize [Device] Storage enabled, the originals still exist on iCloud.

My Photo Stream

My Photo Stream takes advantage of iCloud by not just uploading your photos to the cloud, but also sending new photos to all of your iCloud devices. If you capture a photo on your iPhone, for example, it appears in the photo library of your iPad within a few minutes (or seconds, sometimes)—no awkward syncing to deal with. Go to Settings > iCloud > Photos and turn on the Upload to My Photo Stream option.

A Look Ahead at Photos for OS X

It's worth mentioning that My Photo Stream also works with Apple's OS X applications iPhoto and Aperture. If you already use either of those apps, you can turn on the feature by going to the program's preferences and turning on the My Photo Stream option in the iCloud pane. But hold up a second.

As we write this, Apple has announced that it's retiring both iPhoto and Aperture in favor of a new application, Photos for OS X. Apple teased an early version of it in 2014, and it looked a lot like the Photos app on iOS. That program is expected sometime in 2015, but Apple hasn't made any early versions available for pre-release testing.

We suspect Photos for OS X will hew close to the iOS app, but we don't yet know how extensive its support will be for Aperture-standard features like extended keywords and advanced photo editing tools. To be honest, we haven't used iPhoto for the last several years due to declining reliability and performance in the application, and we only fleetingly dip into Aperture when needed. If you're currently invested in either app, now is the time to start looking at alternatives such as Adobe Lightroom—but it's not the time to panic. Apple has updated both iPhoto and Aperture to work with Yosemite, so we suspect the apps will be supported at least another year until the next version of OS X appears.

iCloud Photo Sharing

Of the changes to the way we work with photos and mobile devices, iCloud Photo Sharing is the one that surprised us as being the most useful. Why? It makes it almost criminally easy to send photos to a group of people with just a few taps.

For example, Jeff created a shared iCloud Photo album to add recent photos of his daughter, and then invited her grandparents, aunts, uncles, and cousins (who conveniently all own Apple devices) to join. Now, whenever he adds a new photo, it's available on their devices within minutes, and all he has to do is share the image once.

iCloud Photo Sharing takes two approaches under iOS 8, which can be used side by side if you'd like.

Share photos with the Family Sharing group

When you set up a Family Sharing group, a new Family album is created. To locate it, open the Photos app on an iOS device and tap the Shared button at the bottom of the screen. Everyone in your Family unit sees the same on their devices. They can view, like, and comment on the photos.

To add photos to that album, do the following:

1. Locate one or more photos in the Photos app you want to share.
2. Tap the Share button (⬆️) and select the photos (2.25).
3. On the iPhone or iPod touch, tap the Next button. (The iPad has enough screen real estate that it doesn't need this intermediate step.)

2.25 Selecting photos to share with the Family group from an iPhone

4. In the share sheet that appears, tap iCloud Photo Sharing (2.26).

2.26 Sharing options in the Photos app

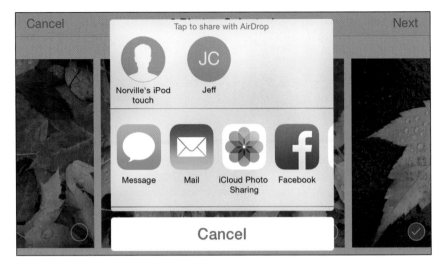

5. Tap the Shared Album link and choose the Family album (2.27). (On the iPhone, you may need to scroll up to reveal the link if the keyboard is in the way.)

6. Optionally add a comment, which appears only on the frontmost image, and then tap Post.

2.27 Adding to the shared Family album (iPad shown here)

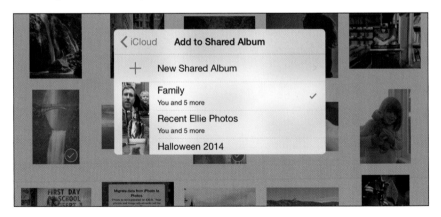

When the photos are done uploading, everyone in the Family unit receives a notification about the new images (2.28). Any member of the group can contribute photos to the Family album.

2.28 The notification other Family group members receive

Photo sharing outside the Family group

Photo sharing isn't limited to a Family Sharing group. You can create albums to share with anyone.

1. Follow steps 1–4 in the previous sequence for selecting and sharing one or more photos.

2. In the Add to Shared Album dialog, instead of selecting the Family album, tap the New Shared Album option.

3. Enter a name for the album and tap Next.

4. Type the name (if they're in your contacts list), email address, or phone number of a person you want to invite to join the shared album (2.29). To invite others, tap the + button and enter their information. Tap Next.

2.29 Inviting a contact to view a shared album

5. Tap Post to create the album with the new photos and send out invitations.

View Photos on the Apple TV

The third-generation Apple TV supports Family Sharing, so you can view photos and slideshows on the television (which beats having to crowd around an iPad or laptop screen). The second-generation Apple TV supports iCloud Photo Sharing.

1. Choose iCloud Photos from the main menu.

2. Choose the Family album (or another shared album).

3. Select a photo to view. Or, select the Slideshow option to view the set as a slideshow. Pick your settings (such as whether photos should be shuffled, if music should play, and a theme to use) and then select Start Slideshow.

▶ **TIP** Choose a shared iCloud Photos album as the Apple TV's screensaver. Go to Settings > Screen Saver > Photos > iCloud Photos and choose the shared folder you want to use (2.30).

2.30 Photos on the Apple TV

Set Up Restrictions

Most of this chapter so far has emphasized sharing apps and media, helping devices play nice together, and generally making your Apple world a better place.

Occasionally, however, you need to just say *no*. The restrictions in iOS and OS X are designed to give you greater control over what kids can do on their devices.

Restrictions fall under a few broad categories. You can limit the applications that are visible, restrict purchases and app installs, filter media (such as allowing only movies rated G or PG), allow only certain Web sites to load, and control which apps can access privacy-sensitive information such as location or Facebook data. On OS X, you can also implement time limits for when the Mac can be used.

Enable Restrictions

iOS calls them "restrictions," OS X calls them "parental controls," but the options for limiting access are similar on both platforms.

On iOS, go to Settings > General > Restrictions and tap Enable Restrictions. Create a four-digit passcode and verify it.

Under OS X, restrictions are set at the user level. Create a new managed account or apply parental controls to an existing non-administrator account:

1. Open System Preferences, go to the Parental Controls preference pane, and select the user account to which you want to apply oversight. Or, click the + button at the bottom of the user list to create a new user.

2. Enter a full name, account name, and password method, and then click Create User.

▶ **TIP** If you have access to the child's computer over the network, you can manage parental controls from your own administrator account. Select the Manage Parental Controls from Another Computer option. That also enables you to configure the controls from your account on the same computer the child uses, without having to log in to their account each time you want to change something.

▶ **NOTE** We probably don't need to mention this, but remember to choose a restrictions passcode that the child doesn't know. On OS X, your administrator account password locks the parental controls, so keep that info close to the vest, too.

Restrict Apps

Typically, any app on an iOS device or on a Mac is available to use, but there are good reasons for restricting access to some. For example, you may not want your child starting FaceTime conversations or browsing the Web.

On iOS, go to the Restrictions settings and turn applications listed in the Allow section on or off (2.31). When you do, the apps completely disappear from the Home screen.

2.31 Choosing which apps and services to be available

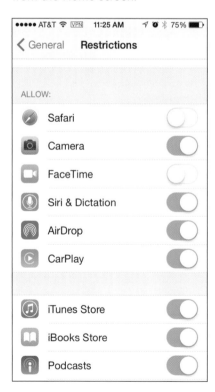

However, iOS restrictions include just a few apps and services (such as Siri and AirDrop). On the Mac, you can filter any application installed on the computer:

In the Parental Controls preference pane, click the Apps button if it's not already selected and then select the Limit Applications checkbox (2.32). The options below are broken into two components:

- The Allow App Store Apps pop-up menu takes advantage of the security of the Mac App Store (since every app offered there is vetted by Apple). Developers are required to assign an age range for the apps, so you can click the menu and choose which apps are allowed based on those ranges (such as Up to 9+).

- The Allowed Apps box reveals every app installed on the Mac. Select the checkbox for any apps you want available.

2.32 App restrictions in OS X Yosemite

▶ **NOTE** Another option is Use Simple Finder, which presents available apps in a window (2.33). Clicking the Documents folder in the Dock displays a window containing just documents. In both cases, clicking once on an app or file icon launches it. Although the idea is sound—you want to minimize complexity—the Simple Finder is a throwback to earlier editions of OS X (and it feels like that). We'd prefer to leave this option off, limit the apps that can be used, and use Launchbar to open the apps.

2.33 Simple Finder

Restrict app purchases and installations

Family Sharing includes the Ask to Buy feature to help curb purchases and software installations, but you can also just remove the capability to buy items at all. On iOS, turn off the iTunes Store or iBooks Store to make them not appear; turn off Installing Apps to hide the App Store. Disabling the In-App Purchases option retains the ability to browse for new apps but blocks purchases within apps (which can quickly add up, especially for some games).

Restrict Content

Let us tell you a story about how young Jeff convinced his parents to take him to see a little "docudrama" called *Sasquatch: The Legend of Bigfoot*. Expecting a documentary about the mythical beast, Jeff instead spent many many *many* sleepless nights scared out of his wits wondering when Bigfoot was going to crash through his window.

Today, movies like that carry ratings such as PG-13 or R, helping parents decide what to avoid. Now that we watch so much media on iOS devices, parents can limit movies based on those ratings. (Ironically, *Sasquatch* was rated G at the time, so Jeff can't blame his parents for the nightmares.)

On an iOS device, do the following:

1. Go to Settings > General > Restrictions and scroll down to the Allowed Content section.

2. Tap a category, such as Movies, to view the allowed ratings.

3. Select the cutoff you want; ratings marked with checkmarks are allowed, while blocked ratings appear in red (2.34).

    Some categories don't offer a range. In the case of Music & Podcasts, for example, you can disallow material flagged Explicit; the Books category can hide material with explicit sexual content.

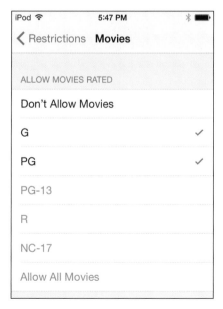

2.34 Restricting movies based on ratings (left) and explicit music and podcasts (right)

On the Mac, the filtering is done in iTunes. Choose iTunes > Preferences, tap the Parental button at the top of the dialog, and specify which content is allowed (2.35).

2.35 Media restrictions in iTunes

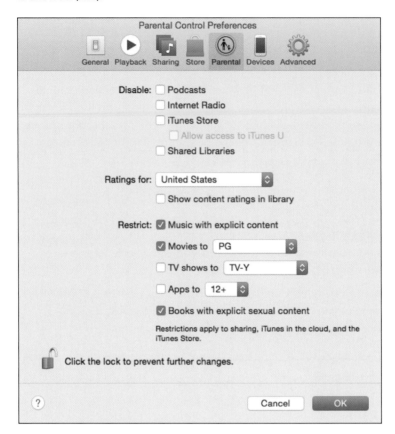

Restrict Web sites

We hate that this is a necessary restriction, but one of the Web's greatest strengths—the ability to publish nearly anything—is also a weakness when it comes to material not appropriate for children. Apple's built-in tools can help steer kids away from corners they're not yet ready to explore.

On both iOS and OS X, Apple's approach is to attempt to avoid adult material—in fact, in the Parental Controls preference pane on a Mac, the option is called, "Try to limit access to adult websites automatically." (On iOS, in the Websites portion of the Restrictions settings, the option is called "Limit Adult Content.")

Choosing one of those options allows you to optionally build two lists: Always Allow to work around Apple's adult filters, and Never Allow, which "blacklists" a site so it never loads (2.36).

The other option is to allow Specific Websites Only, which provides a hand-picked set of sites Apple recommends plus the ability for you to specify sites.

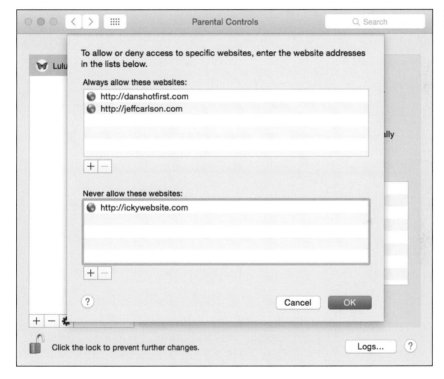

2.36 Allowing and blocking Web sites

Privacy

In the context of parental controls, privacy refers to whether apps on iOS can do things such as access your photos, contacts, calendar items, location information, and more. Go to Settings > General > Restrictions and scroll down to the Privacy section.

For each category, choose Allow Changes or Don't Allow Changes. Selecting Don't Allow Changes doesn't prevent apps that have already been granted access; instead, it locks the settings for those apps and prevents new apps from being added to the list (2.37).

2.37 Restricting which apps can access the Photos library

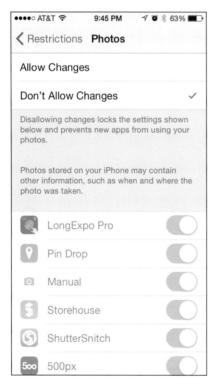

Under OS X, those controls are found in the Security & Privacy preference pane under the Privacy tab. Although they don't fall under the purview of Parental Controls, you as administrator can lock the settings so the child doesn't tamper with them.

People

Both iOS and OS X include controls for interacting with Game Center, Apple's framework for social gaming. In the Restrictions settings on iOS, scroll down to the Game Center section and choose whether the child can join multiplayer games and add new Game Center friends.

Under OS X, the same options appear in the People tab, along with limits for who the child can send and receive email and text messages with (2.38).

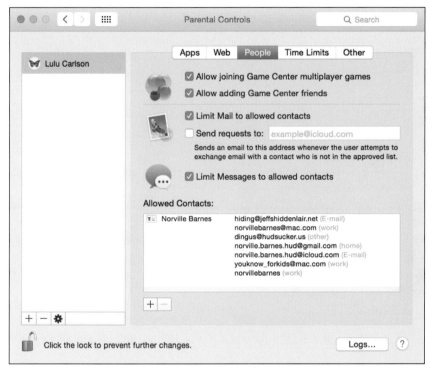

2.38 People-related parental controls in OS X

Time Limits (OS X)

Limiting the amount of time children are exposed to screens is a common concern. In Yosemite's Parental Controls preference pane, click the Time Limits tab to set the number of hours the Mac can be used on weekdays and weekends (2.39, on the next page).

2.39 Setting time limits for when the Mac can be used

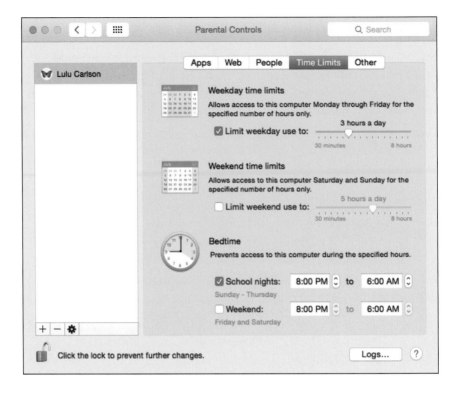

Under Bedtime, you can also specify hours during which the computer or user account is inaccessible (2.40). (With an administrator name and password, you can override the time lock and grant additional hours, such as for late-night homework.)

2.40 Trying to switch to a user on the same Mac that has time limit controls applied

Access Logs (OS X)

OS X also keeps track of Web sites visited, sites blocked, applications run, and conversations in Messages, which the administrator can view in case you feel the need to check up on the child's activity. Click the Logs button in the Parental Controls preference pane to view the information.

Parental Control Strategies

When we set out to write this book, we asked friends about how they managed their kids' access to computers and devices. Restrictions and parental controls provide mechanisms for nudging behavior in the right direction, but parents can't assume that computer settings are adequate to do the whole job. Although we'd love to provide a list of surefire solutions, they don't apply in all cases. But here are some approaches that people recommend.

- Draft and sign a contract. We know it sounds legalistic, but create a contract that spells out exactly what's allowed on a device (such as under which circumstances games can be played), and spell out consequences if the terms are broken. Texting someone the parents don't know? The iPhone is handed over for a week.

- Limit screen time consistently. Establish how much time can be spent on devices or in front of the TV and stick to it.

- Invest in other software. One friend recommended Mobicip (mobicip.com), which appears to take a more comprehensive approach to parental controls than Apple's built-in tools.

- All devices charge in one spot. iPhones, iPads, and portable Macs all need to be recharged, so several people reported that devices get plugged in to a central location after school (or at bedtime) and aren't touched until the next morning.

- Model the behavior you want to see. If you want the kids to stay off mobile devices during dinner, don't sneak a look at your own phone. They pay attention.

- Communicate. Admittedly, this is the most nebulous bullet in this list, but communicate with your kids about what's appropriate, what's dangerous, and what's encouraged in respect to using devices.

CHAPTER 3

Communicate

Families are increasingly far-flung these days, but staying in touch with relatives or friends over long (or short) distances is one task at which technology excels. An iPhone makes and receives phone calls, sure, but if you're like us, the "phone" portion of the device is the communication tool that gets used the least. Texting via Messages enables short, easy bursts of conversation, now accentuated with features such as sending brief audio clips, managing group conversations, and selectively sharing your location with someone else. Video chatting, which was once either science fiction or the bastion of corporate conference rooms, is now a way for regular people to stay connected.

And now, Apple has even circled back on phone calls: With recent models, when a call comes in to your iPhone, you can answer it on your Mac or iPad—or initiate a call from either device—while the iPhone sits in a bag or across the room. A variety of apps from Apple and third parties make it easy for you to keep up to date with your family, no matter where they are.

Text Messaging

One of Jeff's relatives had no interest in buying a smartphone until her friends started regularly sending her text messages. Although her basic cell phone could send and receive texts, in practice doing so was a frustrating mess of coaxing words from the traditional phone numeric keypad.

Apple's Messages app, on both iOS and OS X Yosemite, is a capable multimedia communicator, letting you send text, pictures, video, and even voice messages to your contacts, whether they're across the room or across the world. It also supports group conversations and other rich media types, such as contact records and locations—more on that in a bit.

iMessage vs. SMS Texting

First, a caveat: Not all messages are created equal. Starting in iOS 5 and OS X Mountain Lion, Apple rolled out its own proprietary messaging system, called iMessage. The major advantage of iMessage is that, rather than relying on some esoteric features of the phone network, it sends messages over your device's network data connection, just like your email, Web browsing, and other Internet traffic. And that means that to you, the end user, there's no added cost. It also means you can send texts from a Mac or an iPad instead of reaching for an iPhone to communicate with your friends.

However, because Apple's system is proprietary, it works only between Apple devices. Pretty much any cellphone you encounter these days—smart or otherwise—lets you send and receive text messages via a system called the Short Message Service (SMS). In general, you're paying for that privilege via your mobile plan, whether it be as part of a bundle such as unlimited messaging or, alternatively, in an à la carte, pay-per-message arrangement.

So, texting with your friends on Android, Windows Phone, BlackBerry, or any other phone platform still relies on traditional SMS, and individual messages count against your texting plan (if you have one).

Certain features aren't supported by standard SMS messages. While you can send images and videos to any of your contacts, the user interface for sending those messages is slightly different between text messages and iMessages in iOS 8. Other iOS 8 features, such as audio messages and location sharing, may not work correctly with those not on Apple devices either.

► **NOTE** In reality, images and videos sent using non-Apple devices employ a protocol called MMS (Multimedia Message Service). However, we don't want to load you up with industry acronyms, so we're following Apple's lead in this case and using "SMS" to refer to messages sent outside of the iMessage network.

Fortunately, Apple does a pretty good job of delineating the two. For one thing, it uses a color-coded system: blue for iMessages, green for SMS text messages (3.1). That applies to the name of the contact you're sending a message to, the color of the word balloon for your messages, and even the color of the Send button. The grayed-out placeholder text in the message field also lets you know whether you're sending an iMessage or a text.

3.1 iMessages (left) and SMS (right) color coding

Set Up iMessage Addresses

You can send and receive iMessages both at your iPhone's phone number as well as at email addresses that you specify.

1. Go to Settings > Messages on your iOS device or to Preferences > Accounts in the Messages application on OS X.

2. Under iOS, tap Send & Receive to view the addresses you've set up on your devices. To include a new email, tap the Add Another Email button. In OS X, click the Add Email button.

3. Enter the email address you'd like to use, and tap or click Return. Messages verifies the address and, within a minute or less, you're asked to confirm the action on your devices or via email.

▶ **TIP** To keep iMessages in sync across all of your devices, make sure to set the Start New Conversations option on every device to the same entry. This helps ensure that you don't get replies at multiple addresses, which can sometimes confuse the conversation threads in Messages.

Send and Receive Texts

To send a text message on an iPhone, simply launch the Messages app (3.2). You'll see a list of your previous conversations, with the most recent at top; select any of those to resume them. To start a new conversation, use the Compose button at the top of the list; either type the name of the person you want to talk to, or use the + button to select them from a searchable contact list. Enter your message in the text field and hit Send—your message appears in a text bubble on the right side of the screen.

Text message forwarding

Your Mac and iPad can't send text messages by default, but thanks to a feature of iOS 8 and OS X Yosemite called Text Message Forwarding, you can now send text messages from those devices via your iPhone, as long as they're all logged in to the same iMessage account.

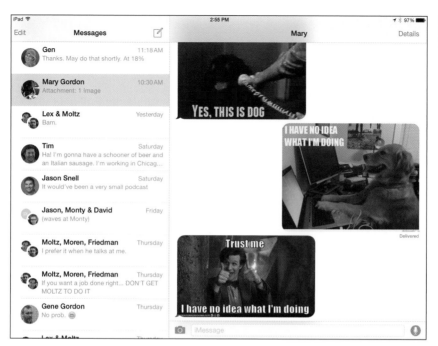

3.2 Covering the important stuff in Messages

In order to enable this feature, do the following:

1. Open Settings > Messages on your iPhone, and tap Text Message Forwarding (3.3). You'll see a list of other devices logged in to your iMessage account.

3.3 Devices that can receive forwarded text messages

2. Tap the switch for the device you want to enable. A dialog prompts you for a six-digit code that will appear on that device.

3. Enter the code from that device and tap Allow.

With Text Message Forwarding enabled, you can send, receive, and reply to SMS messages from Messages on your Mac and/or iPad just as you would from your iPhone, and conversations should be synced between those devices just like normal iMessages.

Images and Video

Sending images or videos via iMessage (or SMS) involves perhaps the least amount of friction of any method. You don't need to hassle with email attachments or upload an image and point people to it. Instead, you take or choose an image or video and zap it off to the recipient.

iOS

On iOS, sending an image with the Messages app is pretty easy, though the interface varies slightly depending on whether or not your contact's device supports iMessage.

1. For all conversations, tap the camera icon to the left of the text field to bring up an image picker that shows a scrollable list of the latest pictures you've taken (3.4).

3.4 Choosing recent photos

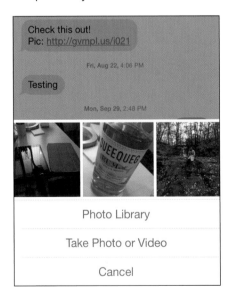

2. Select one or more photos by tapping them.

3. Tap the Send Photo(s) button that appears below the photos. There's also an option to select a photo or video from your device's library, or take a photo or video on the spot. If you tap the Add Comment button, the image appears in the message window; type your comment and then tap Send.

Starting in iOS 8, iMessage-based conversations feature a quicker way to take a photo or video:

1. Touch and hold the camera icon, which summons a radial menu and activates the camera (3.5).

3.5 Spontaneous breakfast update using the radial menu

2. If needed, tap the camera selection button in the upper-right corner to switch between the front and rear cameras.

3. Lift your finger and then tap the camera or video button to capture an image or clip. The media is sent immediately, so for selfies, make sure you check your hair first.

▶ **TIP** While you can lift your finger off the phone after bringing up that menu, you can also simply slide your finger over to either the camera shutter or record button to trigger that particular function—though be warned that the image or video will be sent as soon as you lift your finger.

▶ **NOTE** For some reason, holding the camera icon when an iPhone or iPad is in landscape (horizontal) orientation does not bring up the circular control pad. Perhaps this is a bug that will be addressed in a subsequent iOS release.

Video messages are automatically deleted after two minutes, unless you or the person you're conversing with elects to keep them. If you'd rather they last forever by default, you can select different expiration options in Settings > Messages under Video Messages (3.6).

3.6 Choosing when messages expire

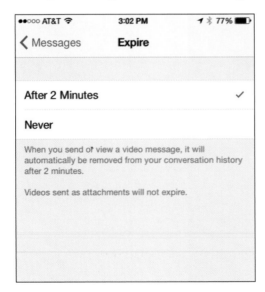

OS X

On a Mac, sending an image or video is a little different. Although there's no convenient button to just take a picture or video (remember, not all Macs have built-in cameras), you can drag an image or video file into the text field and hit the Return key.

Alternatively, go to the Buddies menu and select Send File to bring up the standard document chooser and pick a file from somewhere on your Mac (3.7).

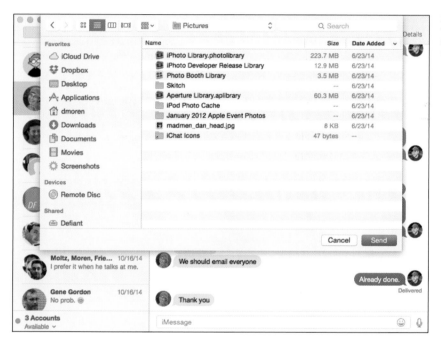

3.7 Selecting images to attach to a conversation in Messages under Yosemite

Audio

Sure, you could simply call someone on the phone, but sometimes you don't want to engage in a lengthy conversation or spend the time typing out a complicated thought to send via text. In those situations, iOS 8 and OS X Yosemite let you quickly exchange audio messages with any of your iMessage-using contacts.

On iOS 8, recording an audio message is just as simple as making a photo or video.

1. Touch and hold the microphone icon to the right of the message field (not to be confused with the Dictation microphone button on the device's keyboard) (3.8). As soon as you touch it, the message starts recording—an audio waveform scrolls across the screen as you speak.

3.8 Recording audio in a Messages conversation

2. When you're done recording, just lift your finger. If you're not sure whether the message recorded correctly, you can tap the Play button to hear it; those that don't quite cut it can be discarded by tapping the x button.

3. Tap the up-facing arrow to send your missive on its merry way.

The process on OS X Yosemite is pretty similar: Again, you'll click the microphone button next to the text field, and then record your audio (3.9). Once you're done, click the red Stop button and you'll get a chance to play back your message before transmitting it.

Listening to messages from your conversation partner is equally easy; just tap the message's play button. Or, lift the phone to your ear, even if you're at the lock screen. This option, Raise to Listen, can be enabled or disabled under Settings > Messages.

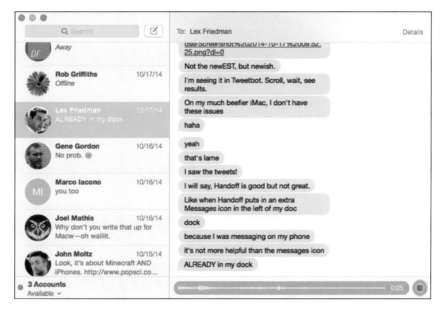

3.9 Recording an impromtu message

Like video messages, audio messages are, by default, deleted after two minutes, unless you choose to keep them. If you'd rather retain them for posterity, Settings > Messages will also allow you to keep them all by default.

Sharing Location in the Messages App

We've all spent time trying to explain to our friends and family just which Starbucks we want to meet them at, an ability that got a lot easier with iOS 8—and, to a lesser extent, Yosemite. Apple provides a free Find My Friends app for iOS (which is covered in more detail later in this chapter), but Messages now includes the ability to share your location information without switching to a different app. You can share your location with your contacts or quickly see the location of those who've allowed you to see their whereabouts.

In Messages on either Yosemite or iOS 8, tap the Details button at the top of your conversation to bring up contact information for your chat partner, as well as a thumbnail map of their location, if they've allowed you to see it (3.10).

On iOS 8, the same pane lets you control sharing of your own whereabouts. If you're just trying to meet up with someone, tap the Send My Current Location button; it does just what it says on the tin.

3.10 Find My Lex using the Messages application

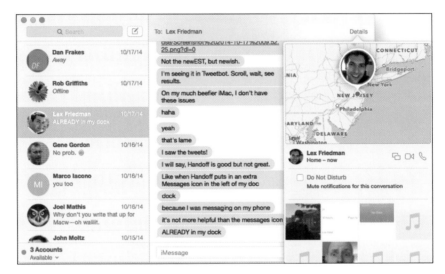

If, on the other hand, you're looking for a longer-term arrangement, tap Share My Location to make your location available to whomever you're chatting with for one hour or until the end of the day—perfect for an excursion to, say, a theme park. You can also choose to share your location indefinitely, and of course, should you already be sharing your location, you can elect to stop doing so.

While these location-sharing features work together with the Find My Friends app, they are distinct from the location sharing in Find My iPhone. More on those features later.

Messaging in Groups

Talking to just a single person is fine, but often you may want to bring more folks into the fold. Messages supports group conversations on both iOS and OS X.

Group messages are a bit like email threads where people are always "reply all-ing." Messages—whether they're text, images, video, audio, or other—go to all participants. Incoming messages are labeled with the name of the sender above them, and if you've got a picture associated with the contact, that's displayed as well (3.11).

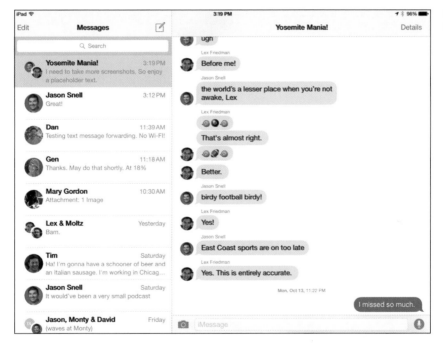

3.11 Group messaging

By default, your conversations are named with the contacts you're chatting with, but you can actually set a distinct title for a particular chat. For example, you might choose to name a conversation with your parents "The Fam." Select the Details option and enter a group name (**3.12, on the next page**). On iOS 8, you have to swipe down after you tap Details to reveal the Group Name field.

To add additional participants to the conversation as you go, head to the Details section and choose Add Contact.

You can also remove one of the conversation partners from the Details screen: On iOS 8, swipe to the left as though you were deleting an email, and then tap the Delete button that appears (3.13). On OS X Yosemite, Control-click the person you want to remove and choose Remove from Conversation. If the person you'd like to remove is yourself, you can choose Leave Conversation.

3.12 Choosing a new group name

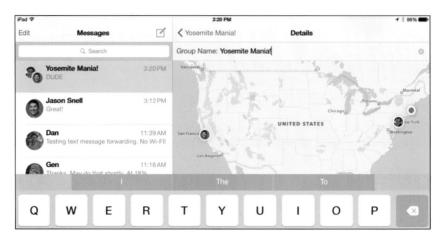

3.13 Removing someone from a group conversation

Since group messages can be high traffic, you might not want to get notified every single time somebody adds to the conversation. Also on the Details screen, activate the Do Not Disturb option for that thread, temporarily muting notifications for just the current conversation. You can always come back later and unmute when you're ready to be bothered again.

▶ **NOTE** If even a single member of your group conversation is not using iMessage, than all of the messages to that conversation will be sent as traditional SMS messages, which can quickly run up against text limits or potentially incur extra charges. If your carrier supports group MMS, which can send multiple messages as a single message, you can enable the Group Messaging feature in Settings > Messages, which can help offset that.

Conversation History

The Messages app keeps your conversation history, so you can scroll back to look at your history or type something in the Search field. (And remember, as mentioned earlier, you can swipe left to view timestamps for each message.)

If you're looking for a specific picture or other attachment, endlessly scrolling through the history is less than helpful. Fortunately, on iOS 8, tap the Details button and scroll down to the Attachments section to view a gallery of every non-text message you've exchanged (3.14, on the next page).

Tap an attachment to view it. From there, tap the screen once to view controls for sharing items and viewing the attachments as a list (including the file size for the currently selected item). You can also quickly flip through them, as in Photos.

Yosemite also gives you access to those attachments under Details (3.15, on the next page), along with options to open the files in the appropriate application or view them using Quick Look, which also provides sharing options.

While your conversation history can make a fascinating time capsule, there might be occasions when you want those messages not to stick around— for one thing, old picture and video messages can eat up precious storage space on your device.

3.14 Recent attachments (iOS)

3.15 Recent attachments (OS X)

On iOS, you can instead choose to have messages expire. Go to Settings > Messages and, under Message History, tap Keep Messages and select 30 days or 1 year (or keep it set to Forever). Or you can clear your history at any time by deleting the conversation from the main Messages screen— either by swiping to the left and tapping Delete, or by tapping Edit, selecting the conversations you want to get rid of, and then tapping the Delete button in the bottom right.

On the Mac, message histories are handled a little differently. You can close a conversation by Control-clicking it and choosing Close Conversation, or by clicking the X button that appears when you hover over one of your threads. However, that may not actually delete the conversation itself; go to Messages > Preferences and check to see if "Save history when conversations are closed" is selected. If you want to be sure that a thread is well and truly gone, Control-click a conversation and choose Delete Conversation to banish it to the void.

Video and Audio FaceTime Calls

When messaging or phone calls just don't cut it—when your kid is taking their first steps and you can't be there, or grandma and grandpa live too far away to visit regularly—video chat can help make up for lost time. Apple's built-in FaceTime system, included on all Macs and iOS devices, makes it all easy at no extra cost.

In recent years, FaceTime has also gained the ability to make audio-only calls. As with iMessage, the major advantage is that this doesn't use up any minutes allotted to your cellular phone plan. Instead, it uses Wi-Fi, if available, or your cellular data connection; in the former, that means you can talk as long as you like for free, while in the latter, it still might help you avoid extra charges.

Make FaceTime Calls

Using FaceTime is as simple as launching the FaceTime app on your Mac (3.16) or iOS device. You'll see a column with a list of the contacts to whom you've recently made, or from whom you've recently received, FaceTime calls, along with the date and time of those calls.

3.16 FaceTime on OS X

On iOS 8 or OS X Yosemite, quickly filter for either video or audio calls by selecting the relevant button at the top of the list. You can also get information about a contact, including further information about a specific call, by hitting the "i" button next to that call. Missed calls appear highlighted in red.

To initiate a FaceTime call, do one of the following:

- Type the name, email, or phone number of the person you want to chat with in the text field (3.17), and then tap or click the video or audio button next to their name to start the call. You can also tap or click the plus sign (+) button to scroll through your contacts list.

3.17 Searching for a FaceTime contact

- Tap or click any recent call to immediately initiate a return call to that person.

- In the Phone app on an iPhone, or the Contacts app on either iOS or OS X, tap the FaceTime video or audio button to start a call (3.18). The same applies to any app that displays contact information, such as Messages.

- On an iOS device, initiate Siri (press and hold the Home button) and say, "Start a FaceTime call with..." and the name of the contact. You can also specify "FaceTime audio call" to make a call with no video.

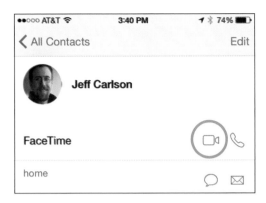

3.18 FaceTime video button

▶ **NOTE** Some devices, such as iPads running iOS 8 and Macs running OS X Yosemite, may also show you non-FaceTime calls, if you're allowing your iPhone to relay standard phone calls to them. More on that feature shortly.

▶ **NOTE** While all current Macs and iOS devices support FaceTime, some Macs—in particular the Mac Pro and Mac mini—don't include built-in cameras, so you may need an external USB camera to take advantage of video chatting.

If you're running OS X Mavericks or an earlier version of the Mac OS, you might notice some differences in the FaceTime app. Instead of seeing just video or audio calls, you can instead filter for missed calls or view all calls, and the app is broken down into three separate lists (3.19): Favorites, for those contacts that you've denoted as such; Recents, for recent calls; and Contacts, the complete list of all of your contacts. To get more information about a call, click the > icon next to a contact's name.

3.19 FaceTime in OS X Mavericks

Receive FaceTime Calls

Incoming FaceTime calls look more or less like your standard phone calls (3.20). On iOS, your screen shows you video of yourself, and provides caller ID for the incoming call. You also get a ringtone, a vibration, or both, depending on how you've configured those options in Settings > Sounds.

3.20 Perhaps this incoming FaceTime call is from Future Dan.

On OS X, on the other hand, you'll get notification of an incoming call in the upper-right corner of your screen (3.21).

3.21 Incoming call on OS X Yosemite

If your iOS device is unlocked, tap to accept or decline the call; if the device is asleep, swipe the Slide to Answer control. In both cases, you also have the option to not answer and to set a reminder for yourself—for an hour, when you leave, or when you get home—or send a pre-written (or custom) text message to the person who called you, saying, for example, that you can't talk right now.

On the Mac, you'll see similar options, though the Reply with Message by default lets you compose a message, and the reminder options are for 5 minutes, 15 minutes, and 1 hour.

Should you accept the call, you have a moment to make sure you don't have any spinach stuck in your teeth before you see your conversation partner, whose image takes up the majority of the screen. A small thumb-nail of your own video shows up in one corner, but you can drag it to any corner of the screen (3.22).

3.22 Position the thumbnail in any corner.

On iOS, tap anywhere on the screen to bring up the in-call controls, which allow you to switch to the rear-facing camera (if applicable), mute your audio, or end the call. On OS X, the controls show up when you hover over the window, but the camera toggle option is replaced by a Full Screen button.

▶ **TIP** If you have more than one camera—or more than one microphone—plugged into your Mac, you can switch between them under the Video menu in the FaceTime app.

To get a wider perspective on the situation, rotate your phone into landscape; on OS X, tap the rotate button that shows up when you mouse over the thumbnail of your video, or choose Video > Use Landscape. (Please don't attempt to turn an iMac onto its side.)

FaceTime audio calls are pretty similar to video calls, but with a few additional options. For example, as on normal phone calls, you can toggle the speaker on and off. You can also add another party to the call by tapping the Add Call button and selecting a different contact. (FaceTime video calls are limited to just two participants.) Finally, you can switch to a video call by tapping the FaceTime button—be aware, however, that your contact will have the option to accept or decline the video call separate from the current call.

Choose Where You Can Be Reached for FaceTime

FaceTime routes incoming calls based on phone numbers or email addresses, giving you control over how people can reach you. In Settings > FaceTime on iOS devices, or in the preferences of the FaceTime application on OS X, choose which addresses are active or add new addresses. You can associate multiple email addresses, but only a single phone number.

▶ **TIP** If you want only certain people to be able to make FaceTime calls to you on a specific device (say, your iPhone), add a separate email address that you use only on that phone.

The FaceTime settings are also where you should define the Caller ID that's sent when you initiate a call. Not only does it help the person on the other end identify you, it lets you control which address or phone number they'll use when calling you back.

Phone Calls from Your Mac or iPad

Your iPad and Mac may not be phones in the traditional sense, but with the help of iOS 8 and OS X Yosemite, you can actually use them to make and receive phone calls with the help of Apple's new Continuity system.

To set up this feature, go to Settings > FaceTime on your iPhone and any other iOS devices from which you want to make phone calls, and enable iPhone Cellular Calls (3.23); in OS X Yosemite, find this option in the Face-Time app under Preferences.

3.23 FaceTime settings in iOS

This option automatically passes any cellular phone calls from your iPhone to iPads and Macs, as long as they're on the same Wi-Fi network and all logged in to your iCloud account.

Much as in FaceTime, those calls pop up on your iPad's lock screen or as a notification on your Mac (and if all the devices are in the same room, it's like a spontaneous bell choir erupts). You can set a reminder or send a message, or answer the call right then and there, at which point you'll see pretty much all the controls that you're familiar with from your iPhone. If at any time you want to switch to your iPhone, simply unlock that device and tap the "Return to phone call" banner at the top of the screen.

The phone connection works in the other direction, too, letting you make calls from an iPad or Mac. Select a recent call in the Audio pane, or enter a contact name or phone number (3.24). If it's not a FaceTime-enabled number, your device will instead make a phone call using your iPhone.

3.24 Dialing an iPhone from the Mac

You can also dial numbers from other apps, including Contacts, Maps, and Safari. In contact records, simply tap or click the phone icon next to the number and choose Call if prompted. In Safari on iOS, tap a number and then tap Call in the resulting dialog.

If you're on OS X Yosemite, hover over the number until a button with a downward-facing arrow appears, then click that and choose Call "[the number]" Using iPhone (3.25). The FaceTime application launches; in the notification that appears, click the Call button. Although the call is being placed by the iPhone, the audio and controls remain on your Mac (3.26).

The FaceTime app on the iPad and OS X Yosemite logs calls you've made, received, and missed, similar to the Phone app on the iPhone.

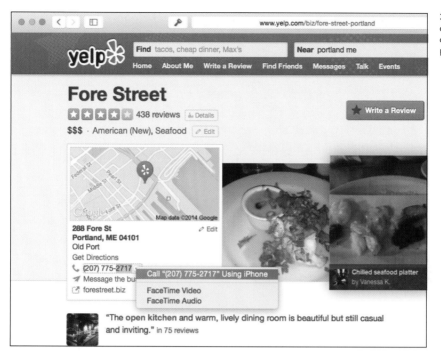

3.25 OS X can determine which digits on a site look like phone numbers.

3.26 A call in progress on the Mac

Multiparty Video Chats

As useful as FaceTime is, it has one significant drawback: It only supports a one-to-one conversation. Granted, if you have several people in the same place, they can all crowd around the Mac or iPad, but if folks are more dispersed, then you can't get everybody together in one big pow-wow.

Fortunately, plenty of third-party apps help fill this gap. Two of the most popular are Skype and Google Hangouts, both of which provide free multi-party video conferencing.

Skype

Currently, Skype's multiparty video-conferencing works only on OS X, not on iOS, but the Microsoft-owned company has plans to bring the feature to Apple's mobile devices as well.

In the Mac client, once you create a Skype account, you need to add the contacts you want to chat with—it's easiest if you know their Skype account name or the email address they used to sign up. Adding a contact sends them a request, which they can accept or deny.

Having jumped through these hoops, starting a video call is as easy as clicking the Video Call next to one of your contact's names (3.27). To add another party to the call, either select them from your contact list and choose Add to Conference, or click the + icon that appears when you hover over the video and choose Add People.

 3.27 Skype

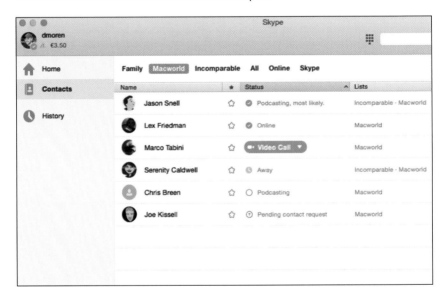

You can also create a conference by selecting New Conversation from the File menu and entering the contact details of the people that you want to talk to. This will start a text conversation, but you can turn it into an audio or video call by hitting the Video Call button in the upper-right corner.

Google Hangouts

As with Skype, Google Hangouts requires that you have a specific account—in this case a Google account—to initiate video chats. Should you be one of the seemingly few folks left on Earth without a free Google account, you can sign up for one at Google.com.

Hangouts are handled through the Google+ social network, and as with Skype, you need to add contacts before you can start inviting them to video chats. Fortunately, Google+ simplifies this process somewhat by letting you create Circles, or groups, of contacts. So you could, for example, add all of your family members to a Family circle. This simplifies matters when you want to start a video chat—a "hangout," in Google's parlance—since you can invite your entire family in one fell swoop.

To start a video hangout on the Mac, do the following:

1. Open a browser and go to plus.google.com.

2. From the main page, open the Hangouts pane, if it's not already open, by clicking the chat balloon with a quotation mark in it.

3. At the bottom, mouse over Start a video Hangout (3.28) and click the button—also labeled Start a video Hangout—that appears.

3.28 Initiating a Google Hangout

On iOS, do this:

1. Download the Hangouts app and sign in with your Google account.

2. Select any of your current hangouts, or create a new hangout by tapping the Compose button above your list of hangouts and adding the people you want to chat with.

3. Once you have a text hangout in progress, convert it to a video hangout by tapping the button with the three dots in the upper-right corner and then choosing video from the toolbar that drops down (3.29). (You can start a voice-only call as well, and even add other participants via a traditional phone call.)

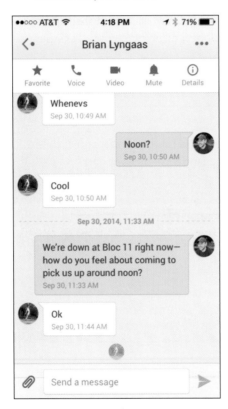

3.29 Starting a Google Hangout from a text chat in iOS

If you haven't converted an existing hangout into a video call, you'll be prompted to invite people to your hangout; start typing the names of your contacts, or any circles (such as Family) that you want to invite. On OS X, there's also a link provided, in case you want to distribute that instead. You need not invite everybody when you start the hangout; you can also add people at a later point if you prefer.

By default, those you've invited will receive a notification—if they have the Hangouts app configured on their iPhone, it should show up there—that they can swipe to join the call. You can also opt for a "quiet" invitation, which appears as a post in those users' Google+ streams.

When other parties join your hangout, thumbnails of their video appear at the bottom of the screen. Google Hangouts automatically switches the main video that occupies most of the screen to whoever is currently talk-ing, so you don't have to scan those little thumbnails to find the right one (3.30). You can also lock the main view on a specific person by clicking or tapping their thumbnail.

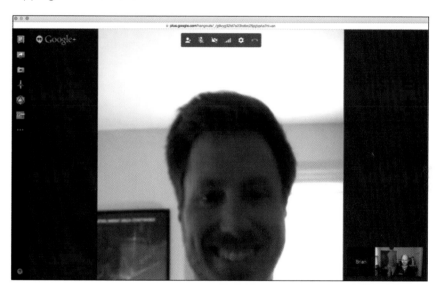

3.30 The active participant gets the full screen.

In addition, you can add other people to the video call, or mute your mic or video. On the Mac side, Google Hangouts offers lots of neat apps and features that you can use in the browser, including games, drawing tools, broadcasting, and more. It's a great way to help your far-flung family stay in touch with a game night, or to share a special occasion such as the holidays.

Location

Back in the old days, you had to set places and times for meetings. These days, it seems everyone has a cellphone, if not a smartphone, enabling people to make plans on the fly. And to make it one step easier, most of *those* phones have location-aware (GPS, or Global Positioning System) hardware in them that makes getting directions and establishing locations a snap.

If you're armed with an iOS device, you can actually opt to automatically share your location with friends and family, albeit with certain caveats. Three apps provide some sort of location-sharing capability: Messages, Find My Friends, and Find My iPhone.

Messages

As described earlier, Messages on iOS 8 allows you to share your location with your conversation partners. In any conversation, hit the Details button at the top right; under Location, you'll see two options: Send My Current Location and Share My Location (3.31).

3.31 Sharing location in the Messages app in iOS 8

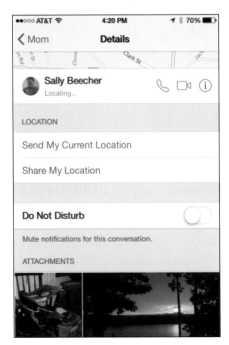

The former option is a one-time action: Location information is sent to your contact, who can then open it in Maps. It's a great way to establish a meeting point and avoid ambiguity when you're at the Starbucks across the street from that other Starbucks.

▶ **NOTE** Although the option exists to send your current location to a friend who's not using iMessage, it may not function correctly.

Share My Location, on the other hand, is an ongoing feature that allows your conversation partners to view your location in that same Details pane until the sharing expires or you stop it. Selecting Share My Location in Messages prompts you with three options: Share for One Hour, Share Until End of Day, or Share Indefinitely. As the names suggest, the first two automatically expire, whereas the last one persists until you come back to that contact and choose Stop Sharing My Location.

If you can't remember with whom you're sharing your location, visit Settings > Privacy > Location Services > Share My Location and get a full list (3.32). This allows you to turn off all your location sharing or to stop sharing your location with specific individuals.

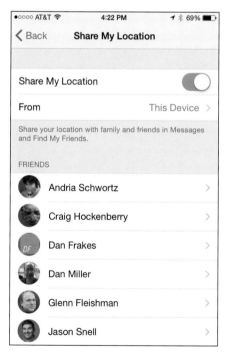

3.32 Who knows where you are?

Find My Friends

Apple's free Find My Friends app for iOS sports many of the same features as the location-sharing capabilities of Messages. But instead of centering on conversations you're having with your contacts, it shows you a map of everyone who is sharing their locations with you.

Your friends are represented by icons on a map (3.33), which behaves much like the Maps app, allowing you to pinch to zoom in or out, pan around, and even toggle between satellite and standard map imagery. Tapping the icon of any of your friends, or selecting them from the list that appears below the map when you first launch, zooms in on that contact. An orange circle around them represents the margin of error for the GPS location, and at the top of the screen you can see how long it's been since the location has been updated (3.34).

3.33 All friends on a map

3.34 A selected friend

Location alerts using geofences

In addition to getting contact details about your selected friend, you can also use Find My Friends to be notified about a specific event, using what's called a *geofence*—an invisible circle around a location—that alerts you whenever the selected contact leaves or arrives (3.35).

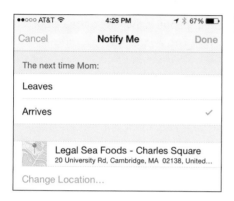

3.35 Geofencing in Find My Friends

Tap Notify Me on the toolbar. By default, you can select it for the person's current location—which is helpful if, say, you want to know when your significant other leaves the house to come meet you. But you can also set any particular location as an option, so, for example, you could be notified when your spouse goes to the grocery store, so that you can text them a reminder to pick up your favorite ice cream.

▶   **NOTE** Be aware that while a person must opt in to sharing their location with you, once they do so there are no further restrictions on features like geofencing.

In addition, you can also set geofences on *yourself* that will notify your contact. If you want your parents to be aware when you set out for your house or arrive home safely, you can configure that by tapping the More button in the toolbar when you're viewing a contact. In the contact record you'll see an option that says Notify with the name of your contact; this allows you not only to create a geofence that will notify your contact, but also to send your location to your contact immediately, à la Messages.

To delete an entry from your Find My Friends list, swipe to the left on the contact in question and select Delete; you will no longer be able to see their location without re-inviting them. You can also tap the Edit button, which allows you to delete contacts or mark certain ones as favorites that will appear at the top of the list in whatever order you choose: Tap the circle to the right of a contact to mark them as a favorite. Members of your Family Sharing group are automatically considered favorites.

To add a new friend to Find My Friends, tap the Add button in the upper-right corner and select the contact or contacts you wish to invite. They'll be notified that you've asked to view their location and given the option to approve or deny the request.

> **NOTE** Keep in mind that Find My Friends is an asymmetrical relationship—that is, asking to follow a friend's location doesn't mean they can see your location. Your friends will have to send you requests of their own, which you can approve or deny.

If you'd rather not receive friend requests at all, you can deactivate them by tapping yourself at the bottom of the Find My Friends list and turning off Allow Friend Requests. You can also turn off location sharing altogether by sliding the Share My Location switch to the off position, and even choose which of your iOS devices you'd like to share your location from, if you have, say, both an iPhone and iPad.

Find My iPhone

Whereas Find My Friends and Messages are concerned with locating people, Find My iPhone is—shockingly—more concerned with locating devices. (The service is also device-specific; you'll encounter Find My iPad, Find My Mac, and Find My iPod Touch for those machines.) If you lose your iPhone, whether between the couch cushions or while you're out and about, the app may help you track it down.

Unlike Messages and Find My Friends, Find My iPhone consists of two parts. The first is a service that you activate as part of iCloud, which lets you track your phone remotely. (iOS will ask when you're setting up your device if you want to enable Find My iPhone.) The second is a free app you download from the App Store, which lets you actively track your device.

To use the Find My iPhone app, you'll have to log in with your iCloud account, at which point you'll see the locations of any and all devices associated with that account that have Find My iPhone (or Find My iPad or Find My Mac) enabled (3.36), as long as they're powered up and have a network connection. Tapping any device will give you a number of options, including erasing the phone, playing a sound, or activating Lost Mode. (You can also sign in with your Apple ID at icloud.com using any Web browser and use Find My iPhone there.)

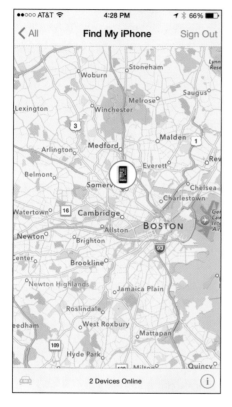

3.36 iPhone found

Because Find My iPhone requires you to log in with your iCloud account, it's handy if someone you know has lost their device: They can log in with their iCloud credentials and use your phone to track down their devices.

Family Sharing and Location

With iOS 8 and Family Sharing, you can activate location sharing with the rest of the members of your family. When you join a family, choose whether or not to share your location with the rest of the family (see Chapter 1).

If you do, it will be available via Messages, Find My Friends, and Find My iPhone. You can turn location sharing off at any time by going to Settings > iCloud and deactivating Share My Location. You can also choose to share your location with only certain family members.

If you turn off your location sharing, your family members will still have your devices listed in Find My iPhone, but without the location. They will, however, be able to play a sound in order to help locate your device.

If you set up a device with restrictions enabled, such as for a child, location sharing can be configured so that you can always locate the device. Go to Settings > General > Restrictions, and under the Privacy heading, tap Share My Location. Set it to Don't Allow Changes to lock the location settings.

Personal Hotspot

If you've ever been stuck in a hotel with pay Wi-Fi—or someplace without Wi-Fi at all—you may have wished for a magic bullet. Such a panacea may not exist, but with the help of iOS's Personal Hotspot feature, you can get all of your devices online anywhere you can get a cell signal.

> ▶ **NOTE** While Personal Hotspot is pretty widely available these days, it may still depend on exactly which carrier you have. Consult with your wireless service provider not only to make sure the feature is available, but also to make sure it doesn't incur any extra charges.

Personal Hotspot essentially turns your iPhone (or cellular-equipped iPad) into a wireless router, sharing its Internet cellular connection with your other devices. To enable the feature, open the Settings app and go to the Personal Hotspot section, then tap the switch next to Personal Hotspot. You also can (and should) set a password that you'll enter when you connect to the hotspot; by default, a random complex password is provided (3.37).

There are three options for connecting to the Personal Hotspot: The fastest and probably most convenient is using Wi-Fi. On iOS, go to the Wi-Fi section of Settings in iOS; on OS X, click the Wi-Fi icon in the menu bar.

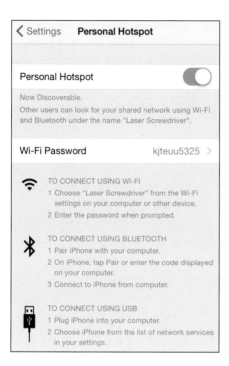

3.37 Sharing a cellular data connection from an iPhone

The name of the network is the same as the name of your device, but with an icon of two interlinked chains—select it, and enter the password you specified and you'll be connected to the hotspot and, through it, to the Internet at large (3.38).

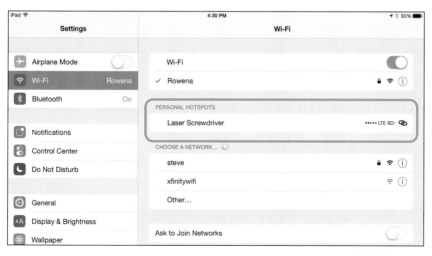

3.38 Personal hotspot available in Wi-Fi settings

> **TIP** If you're running iOS 8 on your iPhone or cellular-equipped iPad, and iOS 8 or OS X Yosemite on the device that you're using to connect to the hotspot—as well as logged in to the same iCloud account—you should be able to connect to the hotspot without even manually enabling it on your iPhone: It will simply show up in the Wi-Fi menu on Yosemite or in the Wi-Fi section of iOS's Settings, and even display the current battery level of the hotspot device. You may not even need to enter the password you've chosen.

You can also connect to the Personal Hotspot on your Mac via either Bluetooth or USB. For the former, you'll need to pair your iPhone or iPad with your Mac; for the latter, you'll need to plug your iPhone or iPad into your Mac with a USB cable, then select it in the Network pane in System Preferences.

While devices are connected to your Personal Hotspot, a blue banner on your iPhone (or iPad) will display how many devices are currently connected. Tapping it will bring you to the Personal Hotspot section of Settings. You can shut down the Personal Hotspot at any time by simply sliding the switch next to Personal Hotspot to off.

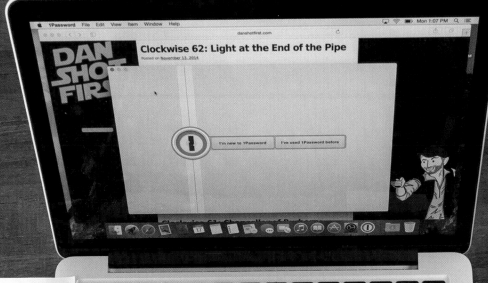

CHAPTER 4

Passwords and Security

"Security" used to refer solely to one's physical safety, such as having good door locks and perhaps a home security system. But in our modern world of hacks and malware and phishing, security increasingly focuses on the important information stored on your computer and devices. You can take concrete steps to keep burglars out of your house, but if a malicious entity steals your credit card information—usually from a hacked retailer, not directly from you—your bank accounts could be drained without you even knowing about it.

Understand at the outset that we're not going to sugarcoat security in this chapter. The days when you could choose a pet name as a password, or use the same password for more than one Web site or service, are long over. Security is now a fact of daily digital life.

The good news is, you're not powerless against these threats. In fact, employing good passcodes, using the security features of iOS and OS X, and making a few smart decisions ahead of time goes a long way toward keeping you and your family members safe from technological threats.

Passcodes on iOS

Set a passcode on your iOS device.

No ifs, ands, or buts.

Yes, some friends or family members may protest at having to enter a code every time they want to use their iPhone or iPad, but it's worth pointing out that they probably wouldn't leave valuables in plain view and the door unlocked when they leave the house.

By default, iOS prompts you to create a passcode when you first activate your device, as well prompting you to enable Touch ID if your device supports it. The latter will certainly be easier for most folks, but remember that it's no excuse for not creating a secure passcode—in fact, the convenience of Touch ID gives you a great opportunity to create an even more secure passcode, since you won't have to enter it as often.

Since iOS requires only a four-digit passcode, entered on a standard number pad, the ability to create a truly secure code might seem limited. However, you can increase the security by choosing a passcode that is much more difficult for someone to crack:

1. Go to Settings > Passcode. (On devices that include a Touch ID sensor, the setting is called Touch ID & Passcode.)

2. Enter your current passcode (because you have one, right?).

3. Slide the toggle next to Simple Passcode to Off (4.1).

This lets you use passwords composed of numbers and other characters, and have them be of any length. When iOS prompts you for your passcode, instead of giving you the number pad you're shown a full keyboard (4.2).

▶ **TIP** If you prefer the speed of entering numbers, you can deactivate Simple Passcode, as instructed, and set your passcode to a longer string of just numbers. When iOS asks you to enter your passcode, you still get the number pad. On the downside, this could alert a potential hacker to the fact that your passcode doesn't contain non-number characters, so you should make it even harder to guess.

▶ **NOTE** A passcode isn't just a door to keep unauthorized people out. When you set up a passcode, all data on the device is encrypted. If, for example, someone were to get hold of your iPhone, open it up, and attempt to access the memory chips directly, the information would be scrambled.

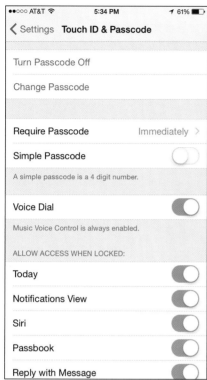

4.1 Passcode settings

4.2 Unlocking with a passcode

Do You Have Touch ID? Use It

Touch ID is more than just a convenient trick for unlocking your iPhone or iPad. If you own an iPhone 5s, iPhone 6, iPhone 6 Plus, iPad Air 2, or iPad mini 3, you were asked during initial setup to scan your fingerprint for Touch ID. That fingerprint image is stored in a section of the device's processor called the Secure Enclave, which, in addition to having a cool name, is inaccessible by other areas of the system except in very specific circumstances. The print is never shared outside the device (such as via iCloud).

With Touch ID, you can verify purchases from the App Store and iTunes Store without entering a password. App developers can also take advantage of the feature—for example, 1Password can be opened by pressing the Touch ID sensor (the Home button). (We cover 1Password later in this chapter.)

You can configure up to five fingerprints for Touch ID. That's handy for using, say, your left thumb as well as your right thumb, but you can also set up a fingerprint for someone you trust, like a spouse or parent.

1. Go to Settings > Touch ID & Passcode.

2. Enter your passcode.

3. Tap Add a Fingerprint.

4. Follow the instructions for placing your finger on the sensor to read it (4.3).

4.3 Setting up Touch ID

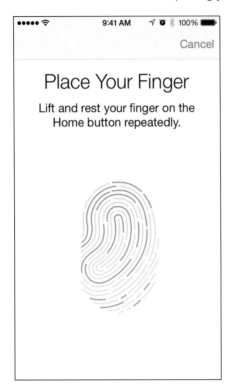

5. When the print is stored, optionally tap it in the Fingerprints list and give it a name that's more descriptive than "Finger 2."

▶ **NOTE** We've heard of a few occasions where Touch ID becomes less responsive over time, although recent iOS updates seem to have improved the situation. If you run into this problem, go to Settings > Touch ID & Passcode, delete the existing fingerprints, and set them up again.

Additional Passcode Options

iOS also allows you to choose how often your passcode is required, assuming you're not using Touch ID. This dictates how long your iOS device needs to be locked before once again prompting you for your passcode. Options range from Immediately to After 4 Hours **(4.4)**.

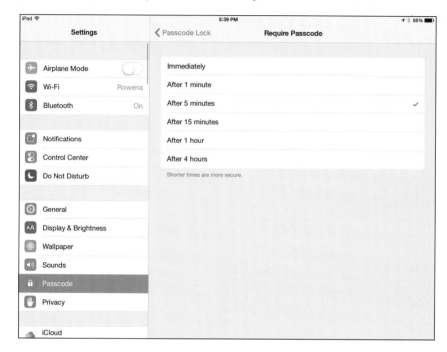

4.4 Choosing when the passcode goes into effect

In general, the smaller the interval, the more secure your device will be. Granted, it can be annoying to have to enter a lengthy passcode every time you want to use your iOS device, but that convenience is balanced against the security of your device should it fall into the wrong hands. For a device that may not leave your house very often—an iPad used by kids, perhaps—you may be able to get by with the After 1 Minute or After 5 Minutes options, but again, if you carry your iPhone with you everywhere, Immediately is the best option. If you've enabled Touch ID, it's also the only option.

The other setting to consider, which *isn't* part of the Passcode section of Settings, is device Auto-Lock, which can be found under Settings > General. This is where you can set how long it takes your iOS device to automatically lock itself—turn off the screen, and so on (4.5). Again, shorter times generally help maintain better security.

4.5 Choosing when the device locks itself

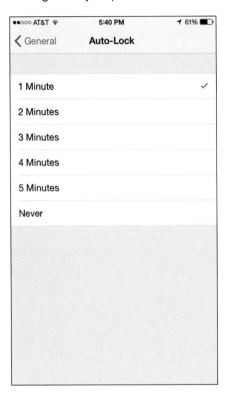

The Settings > Passcode section also allows you to control whether or not certain features are active on your iOS device when it's locked. On the iPad, this includes features like the Today and Notifications views of Notification Center and Siri; on the iPhone, it also includes the Reply with Message function when you receive a call, and Passbook.

Finally, if your iOS device contains particularly sensitive data, or you are very concerned about nobody getting access to your information, you can enable the Erase Data option, which will delete all content on your device after 10 incorrect passcodes are entered.

▶   **TIP** The Erase Data option is particularly unforgiving. Keep in mind that if your household contains, say, a young child who might have access to your iOS device and may try to guess your passcode or even enter random information, you could end up with a wiped device pretty quickly.

The Elements of a Good Passcode

Password hygiene is important, and iOS device passcodes are no exception. In fact, given that most of us carry our iPhones with us wherever we go, and that they often contain access to our email, contacts, text messages, and banking and other accounts, it's even more critical that they be well protected.

A good password is, ideally:

- **Easy to remember.** Having a password so complicated that it must be written down defeats the very point of a password. Using letters, numbers, and special characters all contribute to making your password harder to guess.

  ▶ **TIP** One way to make an easy to remember password is to take a phrase, song lyric, or quote, and use the first letter of each word and then add on a piece of punctuation and a number. For example, "Help me, Obi-wan Kenobi, you're my only hope!" could become "hmokymoh!4".

- **Hard to guess.** As tempting as it might be to use your pet's name, your birthday, or your mother's maiden name, all of these facts are surprisingly easy to find with just a modicum of Internet research.

- **Not reused.** The passcode you use to open your iPhone shouldn't be the same as what you use on any other site or service.

But wait, you may be saying, didn't we argue at the beginning of this chapter to *not* choose passwords that are easy to remember? You're correct! In this case, we're talking only about choosing the passcode that unlocks your device. When it comes to passwords for Web sites and services—especially critical accounts such as your bank or other financial sites—you want the security that a truly randomly generated password provides. We go into that later in this chapter.

Mac Security

Passwords are, of course, no less important on OS X. Again, how seriously you take security may depend on a number of factors, such as whether your Mac is a desktop or laptop, where it's located, who has access to it, and what information is stored on it. A computer left in your living room, to which all of your family members have access, for example, likely has different expectations of privacy and security than a personal laptop used for work.

User security

Mac security is managed in a couple different places in OS X. The Users & Groups preference pane in System Preferences lets you create users with different levels of privilege. In general, if your computer is in use by more than one person, it's a good idea to create multiple accounts, both for the convenient use of certain features and for security.

▶ **TIP** Even if you're the only person using your computer, it's useful to create a new user account that remains basic for testing. If something is crashing under your regular user account, for example, you can restart the computer using the test account and see if the problem persists. It's a good way to see if any background processes (applications that run behind the scenes) are causing the issue.

To create a new account, do the following:

1. Open System Preferences and click the Users & Groups button.

2. Click the Add (+) button at the bottom of the user list. You may need to first click the lock icon below the list and provide your current administrator password to enable the Add button.

3. From the New Account pop-up menu, choose one of four types of user accounts: Administrator, Standard, Managed Account with Parental Controls, and Sharing Only **(4.6)**. The Standard account suffices for most common uses, although certain tasks—some software installation, for example—require that an administrator's password be provided. A managed account allows another user, such as a parent, to restrict exactly which features, functions, and capabilities are available. (You can also convert a Standard account to an Administrator or Managed Account after the fact, or vice versa.)

4. Enter the user's full name; an account name is provided automatically based on what you typed, but you can change that if you want.

5. Under OS X Yosemite, you can choose whether or not an account's password should be the same as the person's iCloud password. In fact, if you set up a new user under Yosemite, the default action is to use your Apple ID. However, we recommend creating a separate password instead; if your iCloud account is compromised, your Mac would also be vulnerable or rendered inaccessible to you. Click the Use Separate Password button.

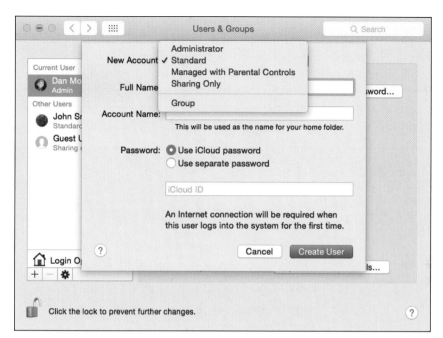

6. Enter a password in the first field (marked with the gray "Required" label); OS X's Password Assistant, the key button to the right, will gladly help you generate one if you need help **(4.7)**. You can change the password later in the Users & Groups pane or in the Security & Privacy pane.

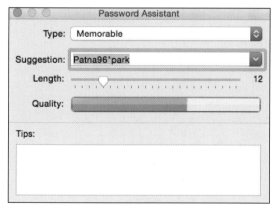

4.7 Password Assistant creates strong passwords.

7. Click the Create User button.

Once you've created a user with a password, you can opt to have your Mac automatically log in to a certain user account when it's booted up, without requiring a password. In the same Users & Groups pane, select Login Options, and then pick an account from the Automatic login drop-down (4.8). This option is useful for a Mac that's primarily used by one person in one location; it's not a good choice for a MacBook you take out of the home or office, since it gives anyone access to your data.

4.8 Turn off Automatic Login on mobile Macs.

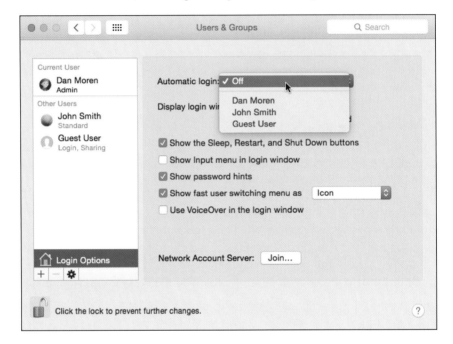

> ▶ **NOTE** If you've enabled FileVault encryption—more on it later—automatic login isn't available as an option for security reasons.

The Login Options section of Users & Groups can additionally be used to configure what's in the login window: whether a full list of users is displayed or simply fields for a username and password. You can also choose to view or hide the Sleep, Restart, and Shut Down buttons, the Input menu, and password hints.

Security & Privacy preferences

Additional options related to passwords and security can be found in the Security & Privacy preference pane of System Preferences. Since it deals with security, the pane includes the same ability to change the password of the currently logged in user as in the Users & Groups pane. You can also choose—as on iOS—how soon a password is required after your Mac goes to sleep or the screen saver starts. Options range from Immediately to 8 hours (4.9). Again, shorter intervals, while sometimes less convenient, ensure tighter security. (You can control how long your computer is inactive before triggering the screen saver or display sleep in the Desktop & Screen Saver or Energy Save preference panes, respectively.)

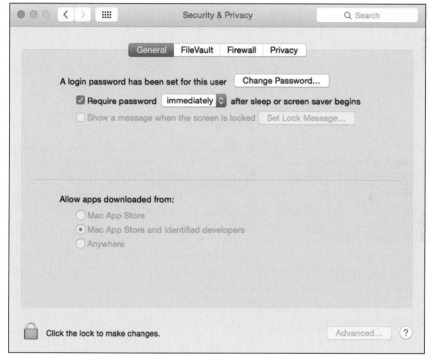

4.9 Choosing how quickly to engage the password request

The Security & Privacy preference pane also allows you to display a message on the login screen, such as contact information in the event that your computer is misplaced or stolen.

One of the most abused attack vectors for malware is convincing people to launch applications that are actually Trojan horses—normal-looking apps that harbor a destructive payload to which the unsuspecting user grants access to the system. Apple's response to this threat is to restrict what can be installed by default. If an installer or an application downloaded from the Internet doesn't match the criteria you specify, OS X does not allow it to be run.

The Allow Apps Downloaded From setting offers three options:

- **Mac App Store.** Apple must approve any software sold through the Mac App Store, so these applications are safe.

- **Mac App Store and Authorized Developers.** Not every company sells its products through the Mac App Store, but Apple maintains a list (which is automatically kept up to date on your Mac) of developers that have passed a certification process.

- **Anywhere.** Choosing Anywhere effectively turns off this line of defense against potentially dangerous applications. It's up to you to make sure the software you install is safe. That doesn't mean anything not authorized or sold from the Mac App Store should be disregarded; it just puts the responsibility in your hands.

Note that this setting applies only to the first time a program is launched or installed. It won't prevent a bad app from running entirely. OS X assumes that if you allowed it to run once, the app must be okay. (A more cynical view is that if you did install malicious software, the damage is already done.)

> ▶ **TIP** We keep this option set to Mac App Store and Authorized Developers to provide a screen of safety, but there's a workaround for installing unauthorized apps you know are safe without making a trip to the Security & Privacy preference pane: In the Finder, Control-click the app or installer and choose Open. In the warning dialog that appears, you can choose to go ahead with the action.

Clicking the Advanced button in Security & Privacy also gives you access to three other security options (4.10): an auto-log out action, with the ability to choose how many minutes of inactivity before it triggers; whether or not any system-wide preferences (those not specifically linked to the current user account) require an administrator password; and, if the Mac is equipped with an infrared receiver, the ability to disable commands from IR remotes.

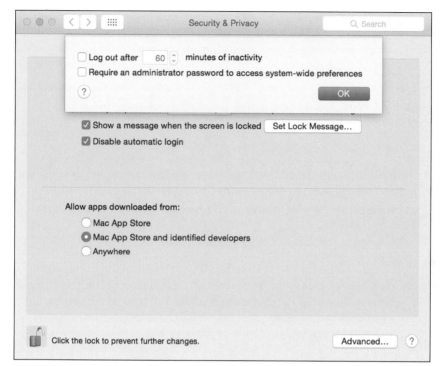

FileVault

Having a strong password on your Mac is a good first step, but what's to prevent somebody malicious from simply pulling the hard drive out of your computer and accessing the data on it? In that scenario, there'd be no need to log in, rendering all your passwords moot.

That's where OS X's FileVault comes in. FileVault encodes your Mac's entire disk with powerful encryption, making it incredibly difficult—if not outright impossible—to access without your account credentials or a secret key you set. While it may not be out-and-out bulletproof, it ought to keep anybody short of a particularly determined interloper out of your files.

The best thing about FileVault is that it does all its work out of sight. Once you set it up, you'll never really notice its presence.

► **NOTE** Not to bore you, but technically the feature we're talking about is FileVault 2. Apple introduced the original FileVault in an older version of OS X that encrypted just the user's Home folder, which turned out to be a cumbersome implementation. Now, FileVault under OS X Yosemite (and as far back as OS X Lion) performs whole-disk encryption.

Configuring FileVault takes just a few steps.

1. Go to the Security & Privacy preference pane in System Preferences and select the FileVault tab.

2. If FileVault is not yet enabled, you'll see a button prompting you to Turn On FileVault. (If the option is grayed out, click the padlock icon and enter an administrator username and password before proceeding.)

► **NOTE** When you enable FileVault, you'll first be presented with two options: to allow your iCloud account access to unlock your disk and reset your password, or to create a recovery key **(4.11)**. While the former is certainly a convenient option, some users may not wish to tie their computer's security to their online account. The recovery key is not stored online, which means you have to find a safe, secure place to keep it, in case you require it later. Both options have their own advantages and disadvantages: which you choose depends on your own personal situation.

4.11 Choose how to unlock FileVault if the password is lost.

3. If you opt to create a recovery key, the next pane displays it **(4.12)**. Make a copy of the key, either written down somewhere secure (a safe or even a safe deposit box), and/or store it in a safe digital location, such as a password manager.

4.12 FileVault recovery key

4. Enter the password for any user accounts on the device beyond the one that is currently enabled. (That, among other things, prevents pranksters from, say, encrypting someone's disk because they left their account logged in.)

5. Once you've logged in all the current users, click Continue. Your Mac prompts you to Restart in order to begin the encryption process.

Upon restarting, you're prompted for your account password. Once you log in, the encryption process begins in the background. Again, it happens transparently; you don't need to do anything, and your other activities shouldn't be affected while the encryption is in process. You can check the progress of the encryption by going to the FileVault section of the Security & Privacy preference pane; a progress bar reflects how much of the disk has been encrypted, and how much is left to go.

Once FileVault is finished with its encryption, the only difference you will notice is that OS X prompts you to log in as soon as you start your computer, rather than once the OS has loaded. You'll see a slightly different login screen—all gray, rather than a translucent one that shows your desktop image behind it.

▶ **NOTE** FileVault explicitly protects your Mac when it's shut down. Once you've logged in, the disk is decrypted in order for you to actually use the machine. So if you use FileVault, keep in mind that you'll still want to protect it with a powerful password and make sure to control physical access to it.

Master Password

People forget their passwords. It happens. OS X provides a variety of ways to reset passwords: Administrators can reset passwords for other admins, as well as for standard, managed, and sharing accounts; if you've enabled it, you can also reset your password using your Apple ID, which is Apple's recommended method for recovering a forgotten password.

One additional option is to create a master password for your machine, which you can use as a sort of override to reset any user account password—even on an account protected by FileVault.

To set a master password, do the following:

1. Go to the Users & Groups preference pane and click the gear icon at the bottom of the list.

2. Choose Set Master Password, and you'll get a familiar-looking dialog.

3. Enter and verify the master password, along with an optional password hint (4.13). Click OK.

4.13 Setting up a master password

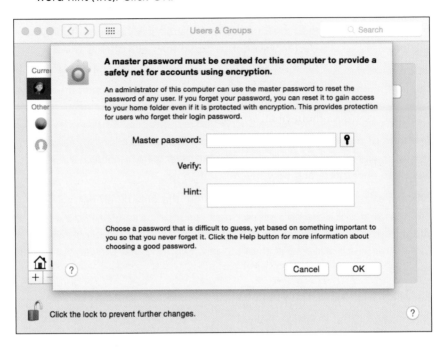

Once a master password is set, if you attempt to log in to an account and fail several times, you'll be prompted to use the master password and create a new password for that account. You can change your master password by going back to the Users & Groups pane and choosing Change Master password from the gear icon, but keep in mind that you'll need to provide the current master password in order to do so.

iCloud Keychain

If you're following good password hygiene—making complex passwords that you don't reuse—you're going to rather quickly run up against the limitations of human memory. Fortunately, OS X provides a solution for not only remembering your passwords but for keeping them all in sync across your various devices: iCloud Keychain.

The Keychain itself dates back to the classic Mac OS, but it's a staple of OS X. It's a secure database for storing all of your passwords for various accounts, Web sites, and so on, all of which can be accessed by typing a single master keychain password—usually the same as your OS X account password.

Starting in iOS 7 and OS X Mavericks, Apple rolled out iCloud Keychain, which lets you sync those passwords—as well as Wi-Fi networks, some credit card information, and other information such as mail, contacts, and calendar accounts—across your Macs and iOS devices, ensuring that the right data is always there when you need it.

Use a VPN When Mobile

If you or other members of a Family Sharing group are at all mobile, you should use a VPN (virtual private network) when connecting to public Wi-Fi hotspots. When you take advantage of a wireless network in a location such as a coffee shop, hotel, or airport, you often hop onto unprotected networks. It's fairly easy for a malicious person to scan all of the wireless traffic for personal information and passwords—that's true even for Wi-Fi networks that require a password.

Think of a VPN as an encrypted tunnel between your computer or iOS device and destinations on the Internet. All of your data is encrypted, so even if someone is snooping the network, they can't do anything with the data you generate. Many companies require employees who work remotely to sign in via a VPN to ensure that potentially valuable work information stays secure.

A VPN used to be a tool that required a computer science degree to set up, but fortunately the real computer scientists are making the tools easier to use. Jeff, who works often at coffee shops, swears by a product called Cloak (getcloak. com), which works on the Mac and on iOS. It's easy to set up, but more importantly, it automatically detects when you connect to an untrusted network and temporarily blocks any outbound traffic until a secure connection is established. The best part: Cloak does that on the iPhone and iPad too.

Cloak is an app on iOS, and a menubar application on OS X, and costs as little as $2.99 a month for 5 GB of encrypted traffic; the Unlimited plan costs just $9.99 a month. (A 30-day trial is also available.)

If you already subscribe to another service, or your work uses a different VPN provider, you can configure the appropriate settings in the Network preference pane (under OS X) and the General > VPN settings (in iOS).

First Setup

If you haven't yet set up iCloud Keychain, you can do so on either your Mac or an iOS device.

1. On OS X, go to System Preferences, select the iCloud pane, and then scroll down in the list of services until you find Keychain. Click the checkbox next to it to enable the service (4.14).

4.14 iCloud preferences on OS X

2. On your iOS device, go to Settings > iCloud, and tap Keychain. Then tap the switch to enable iCoud Keychain (4.15).

4.15 Enabling iCloud Keychain on iOS

3. In both cases, you'll be prompted for your Apple ID password, and then asked to create an iCloud Security Code.

   By default, this code is a four-digit number, much like the passcode you might use for your iOS device. Using the Advanced options, you can also choose to get a random passcode or use a complex alphanumeric code. You can also opt to not create a security code at all: If you do so, Apple won't back your iCloud Keychain up to its server, which also means the company can't help you recover your keychain if it's damaged or otherwise becomes inaccessible. (Keep in mind that your keychain is stored on Apple's servers in encrypted form—the company never has access to your passwords, so it cannot retrieve them for you; the best it can do is help you restore your encrypted data.) However, iCloud Keychain information will continue to sync between devices that you've approved.

4. Enter an SMS-capable phone number at which you can receive verification codes via text. If you need to change this number later, you can do so on OS X via the Options button in the iCloud system preference pane, or on iOS via Settings > iCloud > Keychain > Advanced.

Subsequent Devices

Once you've set up iCloud Keychain on one device, adding other devices is fairly straightforward. Follow the same steps to get to the iCloud settings of System Preferences (OS X) or Settings (iOS) and enable iCloud Keychain. You're then asked to approve the new device from an existing device that's already set up on iCloud Keychain (4.16). A dialog appears on other devices already associated with iCloud Keychain, notifying you that a new device is seeking approval, along with a prompt to enter your iCloud password (4.17).

4.16 Approving iCloud Keychain setup

4.17 Approval occurs on a separate device.

In those cases, you also have the option to approve a new device by entering the iCloud security code that you created, along with a verification code sent via SMS (4.18). While this might seem like a lot of steps to jump through, it's not unwarranted, given the amount of access it provides.

4.18 iCloud security code

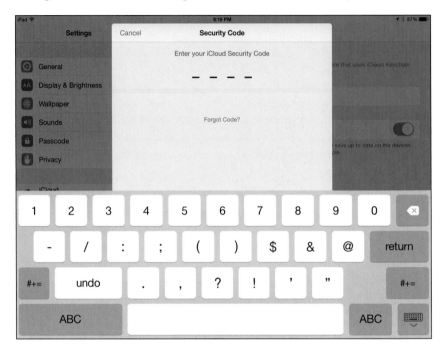

Using iCloud Keychain

The primary place you'll likely encounter iCloud Keychain is Safari, though third-party apps can also connect with it. On OS X, you can also interact with it via the Keychain Access utility. Mostly, that interaction involves filling in usernames and passwords, but your iCloud Keychain can also store and recall credit card information.

Usernames and passwords in iCloud Keychain

On either platform, when you encounter a username and password field in Safari and enter your credentials, a dialog asks if you want to save that password to your keychain (4.19). Doing so makes that information available on any other device using iCloud Keychain.

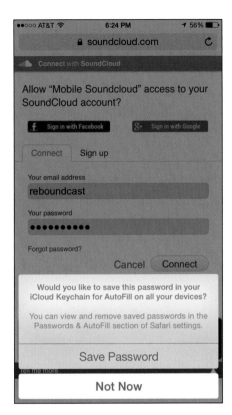

4.19 Saving a site password to iCloud Keychain

To fill in those passwords later, enable AutoFill. On OS X, go to the Safari menu and choose Preferences. Click AutoFill and click the box next to "user names and passwords." **(4.20)** (You can also go to the Passwords section and select the checkbox next to AutoFill User Names and Passwords.)

4.20 Choosing AutoFill sources from iCloud Keychain

On iOS, go to Settings > Safari > Passwords & AutoFill and activate the slider next to Names and Passwords if it isn't already enabled (4.21).

4.21 Enabling AutoFill in Safari for iOS

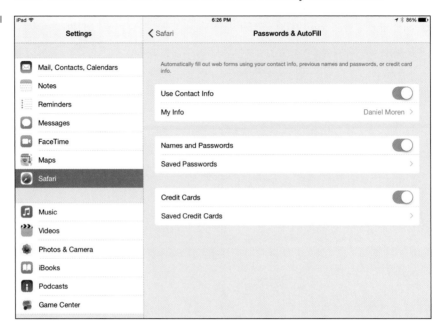

You can view or remove existing passwords from these locations, though it may require your passcode on iOS, and your username and password on OS X.

When Safari on iOS or OS X detects a site for which you've stored a username and password in your keychain, Safari automatically populates that information in the fields provided, which are highlighted in yellow. (If your keychain contains more than one username for that site, it provides a drop-down letting you pick which is the correct one (4.22).) In most cases, you can simply log in without any further intervention.

4.22 Multiple options for filling in username and password fields

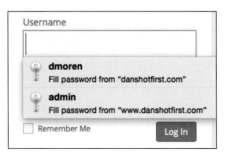

Sometimes, however, you may need to manually trigger AutoFill if Safari can't detect the field in question. On iOS, select a field and tap the Auto-Fill button that appears above the keyboard (4.23). On OS X, you may need to click the field—sometimes Safari will then display an AutoFill dropdown.

4.23 AutoFill fields in OS X

Credit cards in iCloud Keychain

To enable AutoFill for credit cards on OS X, go to the AutoFill section of Safari's Preferences and click the box next to credit cards (4.24, **on the next page**); on iOS, you'll find the option available in the Passwords & AutoFill section of Safari's settings. You can view or remove existing cards as well as add new cards here; to do any of those things on iOS, you'll have to enter your passcode—on OS X, you'll need to enter your username and password only to view an existing card's details.

4.24 Adding credit cards to AutoFill

4.24 Adding credit cards to AutoFill

For security reasons, Safari doesn't automatically populate credit card payments fields, even if you've stored a credit card in your keychain. You can tap the AutoFill button on iOS or click the field in OS X to enter that information, or choose from multiple cards if you have more than one.

▶ **NOTE** iCloud Keychain does not store the security code that appears on the back of your card—that makes it harder for someone to make unauthorized purchases if they compromise your keychain.

Removing a Device

Removing one of your devices from iCloud Keychain is as easy as revisiting System Preferences or Settings and deselecting or disabling iCloud Keychain. You're asked whether you'd like to keep the information currently stored on your device (4.25). If you retain that data, you can still use it, but it ceases updating between that device and your other devices.

4.25 Choosing what to do with stored data after turning off iCloud Keychain

THE CONNECTED APPLE FAMILY

If at any time you want to bring that device back into the iCloud Keychain fold, simply re-enable it following the steps mentioned earlier. To delete your iCloud Keychain data from Apple's servers, delete your iCloud Security Code and remove all your devices from iCloud Keychain.

1Password

iCloud Keychain is a great solution for syncing your passwords: it's built into every Mac and iOS device, it works over iCloud, and it's free. But although it takes care of most basic password-storage needs, some folks will want a tool with more features or which allows use on non-Apple platforms.

Enter password managers. Several excellent third-party apps and services let you store passwords and other secure information for all of your accounts. Among the best is 1Password from Agile Bits, which is available for OS X from the developers' site or the Mac App Store, and on iOS from the App Store as a free download, though certain advanced features require an in-app purchase. You can use 1Password on just the Mac or just on iOS, but being able to sync data increases its usefulness exponentially.

We've used 1Password for years, before Apple implemented iCloud Keychain, so we have a lot of passwords and other information already stored. However, we don't ignore iCloud Keychain—it's better to have two secure options for important data than just one. Also, 1Password includes a few features iCloud Keychain doesn't.

In the Vault

1Password operates on the conceit of secure vaults (4.26). You create a vault, secured with a single master password, in which you store all your credentials for Web sites, account logins, credit cards, software licenses, and more. That way, the only thing you have to remember is the master password.

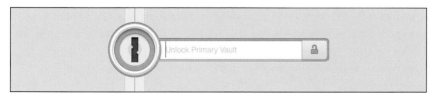

4.26 1Password on the Mac

When you open the app, you're prompted to create your first secure vault and specify a master password (4.27). Obviously, you'll want this master password to be especially memorable and secure, since it's the one password you'll want to remember. (And remember to make it distinct from your OS X account password, because reusing the same password is a no-no.)

Once you've created your vault, start adding items. By default, 1Password offers a handful of common categories, including logins, secure notes, credit cards, and identities. Each of these comes preset with a number of fields tuned for that category of item. But if you tap or click the plus button to add a new item, you'll see a bunch of additional options, everything from your social security number to your outdoor license (4.28).

All of these items are fully searchable from within 1Password—except for the password field—just in case you remember, say, a URL, but not the name of the site. You can also organize your items into folders or tag them if you prefer, as well as mark the items that you find yourself frequently referring to as favorites.

On the Mac, 1Password even supports Smart Folders, letting you dynamically select items based on criteria that you specify—so, for example, if you want to see all the Web site passwords that haven't been updated in a year.

Though, honestly, you don't even have to go to that much trouble, because 1Password for OS X also has a Security Audit feature (4.29). This collects a variety of Smart Folders that not only let you quickly filter for passwords based on age, but also identify weak and duplicate passwords. And the Watchtower feature alerts you to sites on which your password may have been compromised, based on the latest information about security breaches.

4.28 The types of data 1Password already has templates for

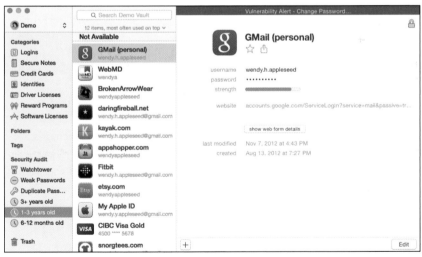

4.29 1Password Security Audit

Browser Integration

You'll probably spend most of your time using 1Password when you're in your Web browser of choice. The good news, then, is that it's extremely easy to use in conjunction with your browser: On OS X, the app includes extensions for both Chrome and Safari, each of which lets you summon the app with a user-defined keystroke. Once you've entered your master password, the 1Password extension automatically fills in the username and password for the site you're viewing (4.30).

4.30 Accessing 1Password within Safari on OS X

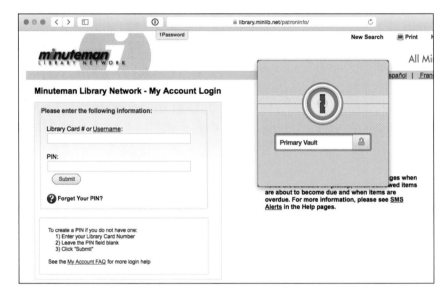

When you create a new account on a Web site, 1Password on the Mac prompts you to add it to your records so you don't forget. And since you're entrusting all your passwords to your vault, 1Password includes a built-in password generator that helps you make complex, secure passwords. If you prefer, you can also access many of these features through 1Password mini, which lives in your Mac's menu bar (4.31).

On the iOS side, you have multiple options. For one, the 1Password app includes its own secure browser, which provides integration with your database of passwords. Just tap the globe icon to access the browser (4.32). When you reach a username and password field, tap the key icon in the toolbar to bring up your password information for that site, along with options for filling in credit cards or personal information.

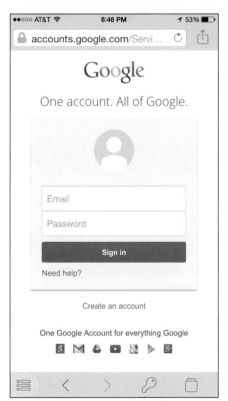

4.31 Generating a secure password in 1Password Mini

4.32 1Password's built-in secure browser on iOS

In iOS 8, however, the addition of extensions means that you can actually access 1Password from other apps, including Safari. Just bring up the Share menu and tap the 1Password option in the Action menu (4.33). If a password is stored for that particular account, tap it to log yourself in, all without ever leaving the app.

4.33 1Password logins in Safari for iOS

Syncing

The real benefit to a password manager, of course, is having all your passwords available at any time. 1Password allows you to sync information to all your devices, whether they're running iOS or OS X—or even, *gasp*, Windows and Android.

1Password provides four different methods of syncing your vault, depending on exactly how you use the app. Choose the one you want in 1Password's in-app Settings > Sync > Sync Service section if on iOS (4.34), or the Sync section of 1Password's Preferences if you're on a Mac (4.35).

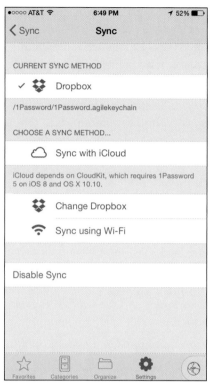

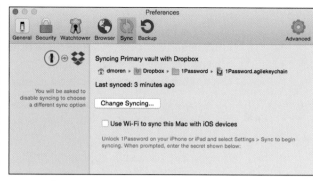

4.35 Configuring Dropbox sync in Yosemite

4.34 Configuring Dropbox sync in iOS

If you're using only devices in Apple's ecosystem, iCloud syncing is easy to set up: Just select it as the service of choice on all your devices, and you're all set.

The second, and most broadly supported, option is Dropbox, which works with not only OS X and iOS, but also Windows, Windows Phone, and Android devices. You'll need to point the apps toward your vault in Dropbox, but once you've done that, it should sync just fine.

▶ **NOTE** If you don't have a Dropbox account, we highly recommend signing up for one at www.dropbox.com (you can get 2 GB of storage for free, or pay for larger capacities). Anything you put into your Dropbox folder is copied to the company's cloud service and to other computers on which you've set up the Dropbox software.

If you want to sync 1Password on your Mac with the iOS client, and you feel a bit wary about letting your information travel through a cloud storage service (even though the data is encrypted), you can opt to sync the two directly via Wi-Fi. Your devices, of course, have to be on the same Wi-Fi network, and you need to manually start the sync.

Finally, if you want to sync 1Password only via multiple computers, not via mobile devices, you can select any folder on your computer in which to store your vault; that folder can then be synced with any cloud storage service, not just Dropbox.

Multiple Vaults

One handy feature of 1Password is support for multiple vaults. If you have more than one person sharing a computer (and they don't have their own user accounts), you can give each user their own vault, secured by their own master password; alternatively, if you want to separate secure information from, say, your work and your personal logins and passwords, you can create separate vaults and toggle between them.

Vaults can be synced independently, so, for example, if you find yourself doing tech support for certain members of your family—and you can convince them to use 1Password—you could set up a vault that you both have access to, making it easier to troubleshoot their problems when they arise. New vaults can be created only on OS X—but they can then be synced to 1Password on iOS. Here's how to set one up:

1. On the Mac, go to the 1Password menu and choose New Vault.

2. Specify a name for the vault, and pick an accent color to make it easy to distinguish.

3. Enter a master password to open the vault, which will be used by you and the other person **(4.36)**.

4. Click Create New Vault.

5. Go to 1Password > Preferences and click the Sync button.

6. Choose a sync method. iCloud can be used only for your Primary vault, so click Dropbox and choose a Dropbox folder to store the vault file. (The Dropbox folder needs to be one that you share with the other person; you can set up sharing after you finish creating the 1Password

vault.) If the other person's computer is on your home network and they don't need mobile syncing, choose the Folder option.

7. Click the Create New button to finish setting up the vault.

4.36 Creating a new shared vault

To add the shared vault to an iOS device (yours and the other person's), do this:

1. Go to Settings > Vaults and tap Add Vault.

2. Tap the Sync with Dropbox button. 1Password connects to your Dropbox account—you may have to grant it access.

3. Tap the name of your Dropbox account. 1Password scans the entire folder to locate any vaults.

4. In the list of saved vaults, tap the one you created in the previous steps.

5. Enter the vault's master password.

To switch between vaults in the 1Password app, go to Settings > Vaults and choose the one you want. On the Mac, choose a vault from the drop-down above the category list.

▶ **TIP** Create a new entry in your Primary vault that includes the password to the vault you created, to make sure you have a record of that password.

▶ **TIP** On the Mac, you can copy or move 1Password entries between vaults, making it easier to share items you have in common (such as online access to a joint bank account). Select a record and choose Item > Share, then choose the vault from the submenu that appears, and select Copy or Move.

Find a Lost Device

Losing a digital device can be a traumatic experience. While the devices themselves are expensive to replace, the information on them is all too often irreplaceable. Fortunately, the same technology that makes these devices so useful can also be turned toward bringing an errant device home—even if it had only fallen between the couch cushions.

Enabling Find My iPhone/iPad/iPod/Mac

The good news is that most of the devices that you might misplace come with ways of locating themselves. iPhones contain GPS chips, while iPads, iPod touches, and Macs can all locate themselves based on nearby Wi-Fi networks.

To take advantage of this feature, you'll need to activate Find My iPhone (or iPad, iPod, or Mac, depending on which device you're using), the service that reports in on the devices' locations (4.37). On iOS, this is in Settings > iCloud; on OS X, the service is called Find My Mac and is located in the iCloud preference pane of System Preferences (4.38).

When you activate the service, you're asked to allow the device's location to be reported via the service; tap or click Allow. (If you enabled Find My [Device] when you set up the device, it's already running.)

4.37 Activating Find My Mac in Yosemite

4.38 Activating Find My iPhone in iOS

iOS devices also have one additional option once the service is activated: Send Last Location. When your device's battery runs low, it'll send its last known location to Apple's servers—that way you should be able to locate your device even if it's out of juice.

Finding a Device

The most important thing to do when you lose a device is stay calm. As soon as possible, try to access the Find My iPhone service and locate your device.

If you have an iOS device available—either yours or somebody else's—use Apple's free Find My iPhone app to locate your errant gadget. (Don't be fooled by the name: It'll help you locate iPads, iPods, and Macs too, as long as you've followed the above steps to enable the service on those devices.)

1. Launch the Find My iPhone app, and enter the iCloud account and password with which the missing device is associated. (On somebody else's device, you may need to tap the Sign Out button and sign in with your iCloud account.) You'll see a map and, if you have more than one machine registered with the service, a list of all the available Macs and iOS devices, along with when their location was last reported (4.39). By default, their locations are shown on the map.

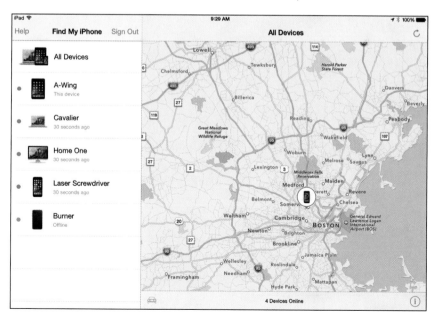

4.39 It's right there. I'm pointing right at it.

2. Select any single device to see just that device's location and status.

Once you select a device, you have a number of options.

- To quickly plot driving directions via the Maps app, tap the car icon at the bottom left of the map.

- Tap Actions to bring up a toolbar of other options, including Play Sound (which works even if the device in question is muted), the ability to erase the device, and either activating Lost Mode (for an iOS device) or locking the machine (for a Mac) **(4.40)**. Play Sound is usually sufficient for us to find where the device has run off to.

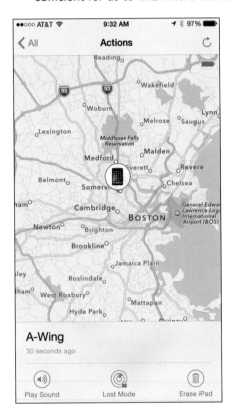

If you don't have an iOS device handy but do have a computer, you can perform all of these functions from Apple's iCloud Web site. Just go to www.icloud.com, enter your username and password, and select the Find

My iPhone icon. You'll find the same options as you would have on an iOS device (4.41).

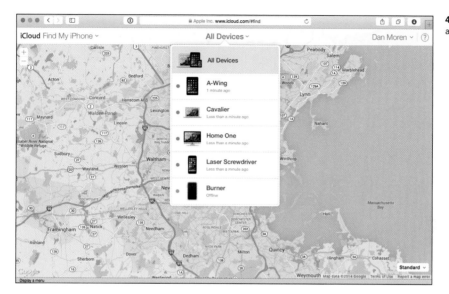

4.41 Find My iPhone at iCloud.com

Lost Mode

If you've truly misplaced your iOS device or suspect that it may have been stolen, activating Lost Mode can help you track it, as well as lock it so that it's inaccessible. Use the Find My iPhone app or iCloud Web site to turn Lost Mode on.

Once you've activated it, you can optionally enter a phone number, which is displayed on the iPad. (If it's your iPhone that you've misplaced, remember that you'll want to use another phone number, such a friend's or family member's.) You'll also be asked to enter a message that's shown along with the number (4.42, on the next page).

Once you tap Done, your iOS device is placed into Lost Mode: The device is immediately locked if it's currently active, and the lock screen permanently displays the message you entered, along with the phone number you provided (4.43, on the next page). If the lost device is an iPhone, a Call button on the lock screen lets someone quickly contact you at the number you specified.

4.42 Lost Mode

4.43 Not all who wander are lost—except this iPad, which is clearly lost. Please help it find its way home.

While in Lost Mode, your device's movements are also tracked and reported in the Find My iPhone app and Web site. Whenever its location is updated, an email is sent to your address with the last known location.

You can update the phone number or message by selecting the device in Find My iPhone and tapping Lost Mode again—you can also use that screen to turn off Lost Mode once your device has been located. Unlocking an iOS device with your passcode or via Touch ID automatically terminates Lost Mode.

Tip If you suspect your device was stolen, and you locate it on the map, don't attempt to retrieve it yourself. Call the police. Security also applies to keeping yourself out of harm's way.

Lock Your Mac

Much like Lost Mode, locking your Mac provides a way to prevent anybody from using your computer if it's misplaced. You can activate it once you've selected a Mac in Find My iPhone on an iOS device or on the Web (4.44).

▶ **NOTE** A locked Mac, as Find My iPhone will warn you, cannot be erased. Therefore, think carefully before locking it if sensitive data is on your disk—especially if it's not encrypted with FileVault (see earlier).

4.44 Locking a Mac remotely

When you lock your Mac remotely, you're asked to enter and confirm a four-digit code, as well as provide a message that is shown on the Mac. Once you've done that and locked the Mac, the lost computer is restarted and you're sent an email notifying you that the computer has been locked to a passcode—the passcode itself, however, is not provided, so make sure it's one you remember or stored in a secure location.

Once the Mac restarts, you have to enter the code you created before you can log in; entering the pin will unlock the Mac. Keep in mind, however, that if your disk is not encrypted with FileVault, someone could boot the machine from an external drive to get access to that information.

Erase Device

If there's really no hope of recovering a lost device, you may want to consider erasing it, which ensures that any information stored is inaccessible. Be aware that erasing a device is irreversible, and once you do so, you won't be able to play a sound, lock it, put it in Lost Mode, or locate it via Find My iPhone (4.45).

4.45 Erasing a lost iPhone

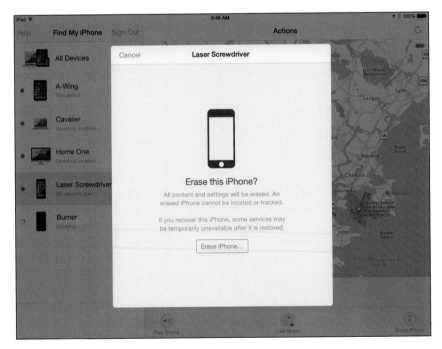

In theory, erasing your device shouldn't be too much of a concern, as long as you have a current backup, either via iCloud Backup or iTunes for iOS devices, or Time Machine or one of the many other third-party solutions on the Mac. You do have a backup, don't you? (See Chapter 6.)

Selecting a device and choosing Erase Device prompts you for your Apple ID password and, as with Lost Mode or locking your Mac, also asks for a phone number and a message that will be displayed on the device after it's erased. In the case of your Mac, you'll also be asked to create a passcode that will be needed to unlock it.

How soon the erase takes effect depends on whether the device is currently online; if it is, the remote wipe starts working immediately. Otherwise, erasure begins the next time the device connects to the Internet. The process of erasing can also take some time: a Mac, for example, can take up to a day.

If you erase a device with cellular service, keep in mind that you will likely want to notify your service provider to suspend the device, just in case someone attempts to use it.

Third-Party Tools

Find My iPhone can only do so much. If you're looking for a tool to help track down the person who stole your device, you may wish to consider a third-party option.

Orbicule's Undercover (www.orbicule.com) not only helps you locate a stolen Mac, but it can also use your computer's built-in camera to take and send pictures, perhaps helping you locate or identify the perpetrator, as well as logging their keystrokes and taking periodic screenshots.

Hidden (www.hiddenapp.com) is another OS X app that, similar to Undercover, can track your stolen Mac, take photos with the camera, snap screenshots, log keystrokes, and let you remotely wipe your computer. It also allows you send messages that your computer will speak aloud, create a reverse secure connection, and more.

Prey Anti Theft (preyproject.com), which runs on both iOS or OS X, is a free option for up to three of your devices. It helps you locate your missing device, as well as providing you with information about the device's use.

CHAPTER 5

Share Essential Information

One advantage of using products in Apple's ecosystem is that it makes sharing certain types of information among devices and users much easier. Apple has put a lot of effort into making its products communicate better than in the past, incorporating new features that emphasize your information over where it's located. There's no need to worry about whether your partner's device can talk to the same services as your device, for example, or whether an event you put on the calendar will show up on your kids' schedules.

A feature such as Handoff allows you to work seamlessly on materials between devices. iCloud syncing keeps calendars, contacts, reminders, and notes up to date—you don't have to worry about where the most recent version of your data is stored. iCloud Drive provides a way to move documents around, even under the fairly restrictive environment of iOS. And don't forget the ability to share your screen or view and control someone else's screen for those times when troubleshooting is best done live and not blindly over the phone.

Handoff

Of the improvements in iOS 8 and OS X Yosemite, Handoff is the one that seems most magical (to take a term from Apple's marketing)—and we wouldn't throw that term around lightly. Handoff bridges the divide between devices when you're working on something and you want to continue on a different device: Take a Web article you're reading on your Mac and load it onto your iPad for reading on the bus, or take an email you began composing on an iPhone and finish it on an iPad so you can take advantage of the larger virtual keyboard. Apple's iWork apps—Pages, Numbers, and Keynote—already support Handoff, and third-party developers are starting to add support for the feature too.

The catch is that Handoff requires fairly recent hardware to run. You must have one of the following Macs running OS X Yosemite:

- MacBook Air (Mid 2012 and later)
- MacBook Pro (Mid 2012 and later)
- iMac (Late 2012 and later)
- Mac mini (Late 2012 and later)
- Mac Pro (Late 2013)

On the mobile side, you need one of the following devices running iOS 8:

- Phone 5 or later
- iPhone 4s (sharing iPhone calls only)
- iPad (4th generation), iPad Air, iPad Air 2
- iPad mini, iPad mini with Retina display, iPad mini 3
- iPod touch (5th generation)

Additionally, each device must have Bluetooth turned on and be signed in to the same iCloud account. To work with Macs, the devices must be on the same Wi-Fi network (Handoff works between iOS devices even when Wi-Fi is turned off).

Here's the magic part. When your devices are near each other and a Handoff-capable app is running, Handoff detects it. For example, if you're composing an email on your iPhone, the Mac displays a Mail icon in the Dock with a badge indicating the origin device (5.1); position the mouse pointer over the icon to reveal the app and source.

5.1 Handoff alert in OS X Yosemite

Handoff email message from iPhone

Click the icon in the Dock to open the application, where the message appears, ready for you to continue writing (5.2). You can also press Command-Tab and choose the app from the application switcher.

Message started on iPhone...   ...and handed off to the Mac to be completed.

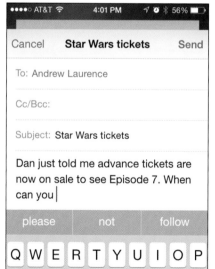
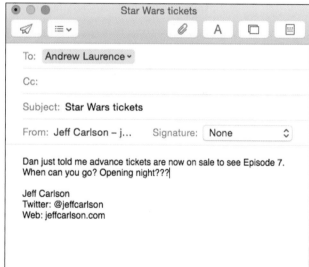

5.2 Handing off email between iPhone and Mac

On iOS devices, the Handoff icon appears in the lower-left corner of the lock screen (5.3). Swipe up from the icon to unlock the device and open the handed-off document. Or, if the device is unlocked, press the Home button twice to view the multitasking display and swipe right; the handed-off app appears to the left of the initial Home screen.

5.3 Handoff alerts for a Pages document on the home screen (left) and multitasking interface (right)

▶ **TIP** If you're not seeing the Handoff icons, and you are running compatible equipment, go to Settings > General > Handoff & Suggested Apps (on iOS) or System Preferences > General (OS X) and make sure Handoff is enabled.

Calendars

Making sure everybody remembers when family game night is, or when you're scheduled to take that cross-country road trip, is key. With the advent of Family Sharing, sharing a calendar with friends or family is simple. And even if you don't use Family Sharing, it's still pretty easy to make sure you're all on the same (calendar) page.

Family Sharing

When you create a new Family unit, a calendar is automatically created and shared between every member of that family via iCloud. Opening the Calendar app on iOS or OS X lists a new calendar, appropriately called "Family," in the Calendar sidebar of your Mac (5.4), or when you tap the Calendars button on iOS. Any event you or someone else in your Family unit creates on that calendar shows up automatically on the devices of everybody else.

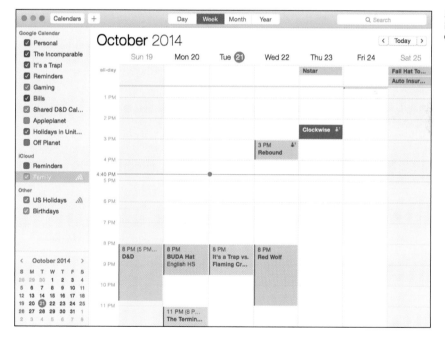

5.4 Family calendar in the sidebar of the Calendar app

That calendar can't be deleted—the only way to remove it is to leave the Family unit, but you can always hide it from display if you need to by unchecking the checkbox next to it on OS X or deselecting it in the Calendars pane on iOS.

To create a new event on iOS, do the following:

1. In the Calendar app, tap the Add (+) button.

2. In the New Event dialog that appears, enter a title.

3. Tap the Starts field and specify the event's date and time (5.5).

5.5 Creating a new event on an iPad

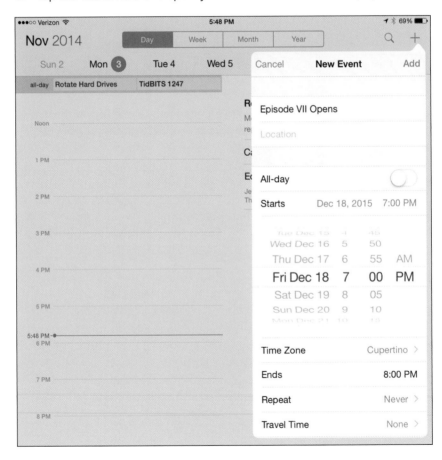

4. Optionally enter a time in the Ends field (the default is one hour), and any other pertinent details (such as whether to display an alert reminding you of the event, a location, or notes).

5. Tap the Add button to create the event.

In the Calendar app on the Mac, create an event using these steps:

1. Click the Create Quick Event button (the + button), and using natural language, type the details of the event. For example, "Avengers 2 May 1 7-10" makes a new event called "Avengers 2" (it's always good to schedule big cultural events, right?) on May 1 spanning from 7 p.m. to 10 p.m. (5.6).

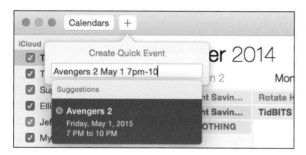

5.6 Creating a new event in OS X

2. When the event appears on the calendar, change or add any details (such as notes or location) in the pop-up dialog associated with it.

iCloud Sharing

If you're not using Family Sharing but you still want to maintain a family calendar, you can share one via iCloud in just a few steps.

1. Create a new calendar either on your Mac by choosing File > New Calendar and selecting your iCloud account or via the iCloud Web interface by clicking the gear menu at the bottom left and choosing New Calendar. (You can't create a new calendar on iOS.)

2. Once you've named your calendar, position the mouse over it in the calendar list and click the sharing icon that appears (it looks a bit like a diagonal version of the Wi-Fi menu). You'll be asked to either share it with certain people privately or make it a public calendar.

3. Given that you're sharing the details of your family events, you'll probably want to allow only the specific members of your family to see the calendar. Enter their names and select their iCloud emails to invite them, then click Done (5.7).

5.7 Sharing a calendar

Invitations to join calendars show up within the Calendar app, just as event invitations do. Click the Inbox button or icon in either iOS or OS X and choose Join Calendar (5.8). The owner of the calendar is automatically notified when somebody joins.

5.8 Calendar update notification

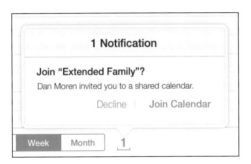

Once you've set up the calendar, any events you create there are shown to anybody subscribed to the calendar. Anyone who has access to the calendar may also add, edit, and delete events.

If you'd like to leave the calendar at any time, simply delete it from your list of calendars. If the owner deletes it, it will remove the calendar and all its events for everybody that the calendar is shared with. The owner can also elect to remove specific people from the calendar by choosing Sharing Settings and deleting the names of certain users. Or the owner can choose Stop Sharing to turn the calendar into a private calendar.

Reminders

For those occasions that you want to remind everybody in your family of something important—say, someone should pick up milk while they're out—sharing a reminders list can be especially helpful. Sharing reminders between family members follows much the same process as sharing calendars.

Family Sharing

If you've already set up Family Sharing, good news: A shared Reminders list named "Family" has already been created for you (5.9). Anything added to this list automatically appears on the list of all family members, along with any alarms, geofences, and so on. As with calendars, you can't remove the Family reminders list without leaving the Family unit. (That might be a bit extreme if you're just trying to avoid a trip to the grocery store.)

5.9 Shared items in the Family reminders category

Shared Reminders

As with calendars, you can also simply create a reminders list that you share with people of your choice. Create a new list in either Reminders on OS X or via the iCloud Web app, and then click the sharing icon (5.10, **on the next page**) beside that list (you may need to hover over the list to get it to appear). Once again, enter the names of the people you want to share the list with, and they'll get an invitation, both via email and via the Reminders app. They can opt to join or decline the invitation.

Reminders	
Mystery Hunt	
Family	.ıll
Shared To Do	.ıll

Share "Shared To Do" with:

✓ Daniel Moren ˅

People sharing this list can add, update and delete reminders.

Done

Once they've joined the list, they're able to add reminders and see (and edit) any reminders that other members have created. They can leave the list at any time, or you can remove them from sharing by clicking the sharing button next to that list and removing their name. If you delete the reminders list, all users are removed, along with any reminders still on the list.

▶ **TIP** When your iOS device is plugged into power, you can say "Hey Siri" to invoke the feature hands-free and then issue your command or question. If you'd prefer that Siri isn't always listening (it can sometimes be triggered based on sounds that may be similar to "Hey Siri"), go to Settings > General > Siri and turn off the Allow "Hey Siri" option.

Contacts

Unlike calendars and reminders, contacts are *not* shared when you create a Family Sharing setup. Apple assumes, for better or worse, that you and your family all want to maintain separate contact lists. If you want to share contacts with someone—a partner, or children, or parents—you need to do a little more work to get it set up.

The easiest approach is actually to create a separate iCloud account whose login information you share between everybody who wants access to those contacts. Although you can technically have only one primary iCloud account logged in, you can in fact sync contacts (and calendars and reminders) with multiple accounts by adding another iCloud account.

1. Go to the Internet Accounts preference pane (5.11) on OS X, or to the Mail, Contacts, Calendars section of the Settings app on iOS (5.12).

2. Click iCloud and enter your contact information (OS X), or tap Add Account and select iCloud, entering your username and password (iOS).

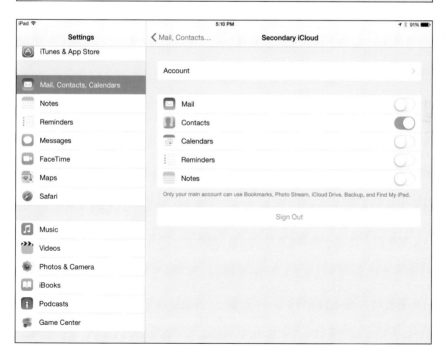

3. Choose which items you want to sync, including Mail, Contacts, Calendars, Reminders, and Notes—note that you can't sync everything your primary iCloud accounts syncs: Certain items, such as keychains, documents, Safari information, and so on, can be synced only with your primary account.

Now that you're syncing multiple accounts in Contacts, however, you need to make sure that when you're looking for a specific contact you choose the right account—or that you search all your accounts' contact information at once. On the Mac, this is controlled in the left-hand sidebar in Contacts (5.13). On iOS, tap the Groups button at the top left and make sure your secondary account is turned off (5.14). Be aware that if you have the same contact in both accounts, that person or business may show up multiple times when you have All Contacts selected.

5.13 Choosing groups in OS X

5.14 Groups in iOS

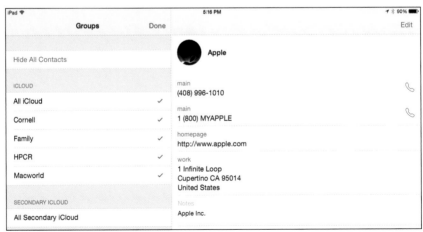

Repeat the above steps for any additional devices to build a synced set of contacts with whomever you choose to share this iCloud account with.

▶ **TIP** You can also use the same process to share calendars, reminders, and notes, if you don't want to use Family Sharing or don't want to go through the process of individually sharing calendars and reminder lists.

Enlist Siri's Help for Events and Reminders

Perhaps in an attempt to appeal to business users, Apple built plenty of calendar and reminder features into Siri. Hold the Home button and use voice commands to do the following and more:

Create an event. Say "Schedule lunch tomorrow" to make a new appointment at noon the next day, or say something like "Meet with Andrew tomorrow at 3 o'clock" to set up a meeting. When you specify a person, Siri asks if it's someone from your contacts list and, if it is, sends an event invitation via email.

Create a reminder. Say "Remind me to do laundry when I get home tonight." Siri not only creates a reminder, it uses geofencing technology to know when you're at your home address, alerting you in case you forget **(5.15)**.

5.15 A reminder created by Siri

Review your schedule. Say "What's on my schedule today?" to hear or view a list of your appointments.

Reschedule events. Say "Change my 11 o'clock appointment to 2 o'clock" and Siri shifts the event; if there is a conflict, Siri notifies you and asks if you'd like to proceed.

Maps

The ability to pinpoint any location and get driving directions on the iPhone has completely changed the way we travel. Having a portable co-pilot that gives turn-by-turn directions has saved us from getting lost more times than we can count. (Well, it's saved Jeff, who has a terrible sense of direction. Dan is aces at knowing where he's going.) When we're research-ing destinations in the Maps app on the Mac or an iPad—where the larger screens aid the search—we can send results to the iPhone using Handoff or the sharing features of iOS and OS X.

Hand Off Maps

Just as you can pass a document between iOS devices or Macs, you can hand off a location or directions.

1. On one device (say, an iPad), search for a location or get driving directions.

2. On the other device (an iPhone in this example), check the lock screen for the Maps Handoff icon (5.16); or, double-press the Home button to view the multitasking interface and swipe right.

3. Swipe up on the icon on the lock screen, or tap the Maps icon in the multitasking interface, to launch the Maps app (5.17).

Share Maps

If your hardware doesn't support Handoff, you can still share a destination between devices.

1. In the Maps app on a Mac, select the location you found and then click the (i) button.

2. Click the Share button and choose the device you want to send the map to (5.18). It appears as a notification on the device.

5.16 Map Handoff icon on the lock screen

5.17 Directions shared via Handoff

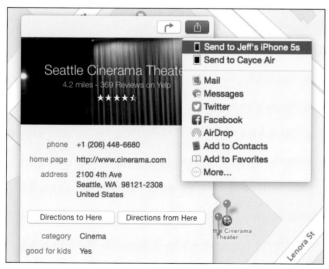

5.18 Sending a map to an iOS device on a Mac that doesn't support Handoff

► **TIP** You can also use AirDrop to transfer a map from one device to another, provided they both support AirDrop (5.19).

5.19 Sharing a location via AirDrop

Share Files with Others

Sometimes you don't want to share something on an ongoing basis— you just want to send over some contact information or a note or event reminder just one time. Fortunately, a ton of methods exist to pass that information along to someone else.

AirDrop

One of the niftiest and most underrated features of Apple's devices in recent years is AirDrop. This technology lets you exchange files and information between two devices in proximity, but without them having to be on the same Wi-Fi network, and without even requiring you to have any contact information for the other person.

And, if you have compatible hardware—an iOS device with a Lightning connector and a Mac from 2012 or later—you can exchange information directly between them too.

On both OS X and iOS, any place that you see a Share button (that box with an arrow coming out of it), you can generally use AirDrop to transfer information to someone else. That includes Contacts, Maps, Safari, and more.

To share something from OS X, do the following:

1. Click the Share button and select AirDrop. Whatever you're looking at shrinks down into a thumbnail on the Share sheet; you should also see any available recipients listed (5.20).

2. Select the device you want to send to; a dialog pops up on that device asking if the user wants to accept the file you're offering (5.21, on the next page). Once they do, the file transfers and you're all set.

▶ **NOTE** If you have a Mac running a version of OS X prior to Yosemite, be aware that AirDrop is not compatible between iOS devices and OS X, only between Macs. Also, Certain hardware doesn't support AirDrop between platforms, even on OS X Yosemite.

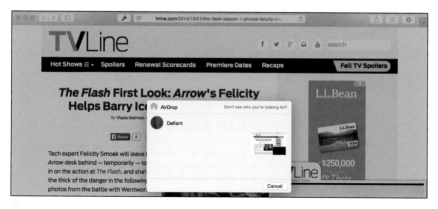

5.20 AirDrop from Safari on OS X

5.21 Receiving a Web page on another Mac via AirDrop

The process is pretty similar on iOS, though you don't even have to explicitly choose AirDrop: As soon as you open the Share sheet, the device starts looking for nearby folks who are accepting AirDrop connections **(5.22)**. Select one, wait for their approval **(5.23)**, and the file transfers.

5.22 AirDrop recipient found

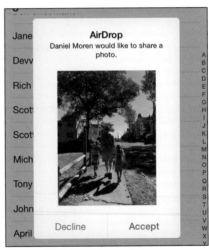

5.23 AirDrop file transfer

iOS users can choose from Control Center whether they want AirDrop to be on, and if it should accept connections from everyone or just from people in their contacts list (5.24). On a Mac, you must specifically open a Finder window and select AirDrop from the menu bar for others to be able to send files to you.

5.24 Choosing AirDrop connections

Files transferred to Macs end up by default in the Downloads folder, while information opens the respective app. For example, a contact opens the Contacts application, while a location opens Maps. The same is true on iOS, although files that don't have a clearly associated type of app prompt you to choose the application you'd like to open them with.

iMessage and Texting

If you need to send data to someone who isn't physically nearby, you have a few options. Email, obviously, is a perfectly good standby in most cases, but then you're entrusting the transmission to the often convoluted byways of multiple email servers around the globe. Instead, consider the surprisingly capable iMessage service and its Messages apps for iOS and OS X. Not only can it handle plain text messages, but it also accommodates photos, videos, short sound messages, contacts, and locations.

As with AirDrop, Messages is available pretty much anywhere you see a Share button. On OS X do the following:

1. Select Messages from the Share menu; whatever you're looking at animatedly shrinks into a thumbnail and gets attached to a miniature Messages dialog (5.25).

5.25 Sharing a map via Messages on OS X

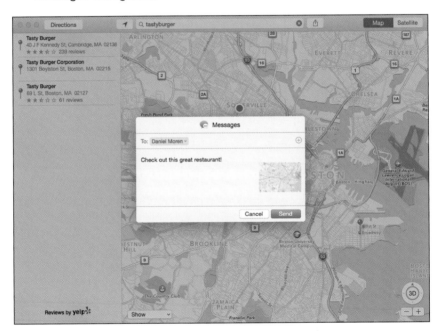

2. Enter your recipients (or click the plus button to add them from a contact list) and optionally a text message.

3. Click Send.

On iOS, the steps are similar:

1. Tap the Share icon and select Message from the Share panel. A Messages window appears with a thumbnail of the information you're sending (5.26); you can enter text before or after it (you may need to drag the insertion point to the correct location).

5.26 Sharing via Messages on iOS

2. Enter one or more recipients.

3. Tap Send, and the message wings its way off to its intended targets.

If you have contacts who don't use iMessage, you can still send some data via text message, such as photos, locations, and contacts. They're generally sent as multimedia messages (MMS), and how well their devices can handle that type of information may vary depending on the platform and device they are using.

iCloud Drive

Apple's productivity applications, such as Pages, store their files on iCloud by default. Until iOS 8 and OS X Yosemite, however, you couldn't access just anything—the documents were constrained to their apps. iCloud Drive opens up that black box a bit, making all files stored on iCloud available in a folder on the Mac and on the Web (iOS still limits access based on apps).

In OS X, switch to the Finder and choose File > New Window, and then click the iCloud Drive item in the sidebar under Favorites (5.27). Or, simply choose Go > iCloud Drive.

5.27 iCloud Drive in the Mac Finder

In a Web browser, go to iCloud.com, enter your Apple ID and password, and click the iCloud Drive icon (5.28).

iCloud Drive also acts as shared storage among computers that can access your Apple ID, much like Dropbox. Copying files to the iCloud Drive (not a specific folder) makes them available to other devices.

5.28 iCloud Drive at iCloud.com

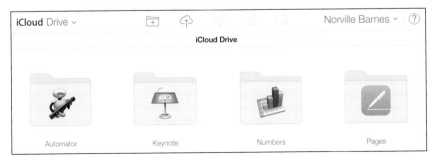

Screen Sharing

Most of this chapter is concerned with sharing items—files, calendar items, contacts, maps—but often, sharing someone's screen is just as important. Believe us, it's much easier to troubleshoot a family member's Mac by looking and controlling it remotely than it is to do it over the phone. OS X offers a number of ways to share your screen or view someone else's. And, new in OS X Yosemite, you can view (although not control) a connected iOS device on your Mac.

Share a Mac's Screen

The ability to share your (or someone else's) screen has been part of OS X for years, although in the past it was a fairly obscure feature. A number of options are available for making the connection.

On a local network

To view and control the screen of another Mac on your network, do the following:

1. Open a new Finder window and select the other Mac in the sidebar, listed under Shared. (The other Mac does not need to be running Yosemite.)

2. Click the Share Screen button. The Screen Sharing application launches.

3. Enter the name and password of an authorized user of that Mac. That can be the primary user account, or an administrator account you've set up previously. The computer's screen appears within a Screen Sharing window (5.29, on the next page).

As long as Screen Sharing is the frontmost application, you can control the other computer just as if it were the one you're working on.

> ▶ **TIP** If you manage several computers on your network, install the utility ScreenSharingMenulet (www.klieme.com/ScreenSharingMenulet.html), which provides fast access to network computers from the menu bar.

5.29 Dream a little screen

Via Messages

The OS X Messages application has a secret: At its core, the application is iChat, a chat utility Apple offered before creating its iMessage service. iChat used the AIM (AOL Instant Messenger) network as its backbone, and those features are still mostly present in the current application. If you set up an Apple ID before 2012, chances are it's also tied to that network. If not, you can create a new AOL account: Choose Messages > Preferences, click the Accounts button, click the Add (+) button at the bottom of the accounts list, and select AOL. Click Continue and follow the instructions to set up the account.

For our purposes here, the AOL account unlocks the screen sharing features of iChat. When you and the other person whose screen you want to share are set up, do the following:

1. In Messages, choose Window > Buddy List. (If the list is empty, click the + button and create a new buddy using their account name.)

2. Select your buddy in the Buddy List window and choose Buddies > Ask to Share [name of buddy]'s Screen. You can also Control-click the buddy and choose the same item from the contextual menu (5.30).

   After the other person confirms the request, you can see and control their screen. An audio chat is also started so you can talk to each other.

5.30 Requesting to share someone's screen in Messages

If you'd like to share your screen with the other person, choose Buddies > Share My Screen with [name of buddy].

▶ **TIP** Another great option for connecting to remote Macs is the app called, simply, Screens (edovia.com/screens/). You install a small utility called Screens Connect on the Macs to which you want to connect, which cuts through most of the network cruft that can get in the way of establishing a connection. The best part of Screens is that its iOS app enables you to connect to Macs over the Internet using an iPad or iPhone.

View or Record an iOS Device on a Mac

New in OS X Yosemite is the capability to connect an iPhone, iPad, or iPod touch to a Mac and view the device. The main purpose of this feature is to record what's happening on the device, but picture this scenario: A friend in another city is stumped by something on his iPhone, and trying to explain it via text or on the phone isn't working. Combining the screen sharing capabilities just mentioned and this method of connecting an iOS device, you can see exactly what's going on and guide him to the outcome.

Here's how you view an iOS device on a Mac:

1. Plug the iPhone, iPad, or iPod touch into the Mac's USB port using the sync cable that came with the device. Make sure it's unlocked (not asleep).

2. Open the QuickTime Player application on the Mac.

3. Choose New > Movie Recording.

4. In the Movie Recording window that appears, click the menu to the right of the Record button and choose the iOS device as the video source (5.31). The screen takes over the recording window (5.32).

▶ **TIP** Another option for viewing an iOS device on a Mac is the utility Reflector (www.airsquirrels.com/reflector/), which makes your Mac masquerade as an AirPlay destination. On the device, swipe up from the bottom of the screen to reveal Control Center, and then choose the Mac's name from the AirPlay menu.

5.31 Selecting the iPhone as the video source

5.32 A live connection to the iPhone on the Mac

CHAPTER 6

Back Up Important Data

Disasters happen: It's a fact of life. And while you can't prevent disasters, unexpected as they are, it's important to do your best to prepare for them. In the case of your computer, that means backing up your data. Regularly. And preferably in more than one place.

Fortunately, there are a variety of good options to make sure that you've got copies of all of your data, for both your Mac and your iOS devices, so that if—when—disaster does strike, you can be back on your feet in no time.

Back Up an iOS Device to iCloud

The best kind of backup is the kind that you don't have to think about, and that's where iCloud Backup comes in. It ensures that your iOS device backs up its data to Apple's servers at least once a day, as long as you're signed in to your iCloud account and you have the system turned on. The device attempts to back itself up when it's plugged into power, on a Wi-Fi network, and locked.

Your iOS device should prompt you to enable iCloud Backup when you first set it up, but if you're not sure (or you had it turned off but want to enable it), go to Settings > iCloud > Backup, and flip the switch to the On position (6.1). That pane also reports when your device last backed itself up, and provides an option to manually start a backup by tapping Back Up Now.

6.1 iCloud Backup

Managing Space

The tricky aspect of backing up to iCloud is that, by default, your iCloud account comes with only 5 GB of space. That may be enough to back up your key data, but when you start adding photos and videos into the mix, it gets filled pretty quickly—especially if you own more than one iOS device. You can pay an additional $1 a month to upgrade to 25 GB of iCloud backup space, or an additional $4 a month to bump that up to 200 GB. (You can also pay $10 a month for 500 GB and $20 a month for 1 TB of storage.)

If you'd prefer not to spend the extra cash, you can also take a fine-toothed comb to the data that you're actually backing up. In Settings > iCloud, tap Storage and then Manage Storage to get a closer look at what you're storing (6.2).

6.2 iCloud storage allocation on iOS

This pane is broken into two sections, the first of which shows backups for all your devices, and the second of which shows you details about documents and data stored in iCloud on an app-by-app basis. The first item in the Backups list should be your current device—tap that to see what information from your device is being backed up.

Under your device, the Backup Options section reveals how much data is being backed up for each app (6.3, on the next page). You can also choose to disable backups for any particular app to save space. Keep in mind that it isn't the space taken up by the app itself, but rather by the data that you have stored in the app (such as video clips and assets in iMovie). It might be as little as a few kilobytes of settings, or as much as several megabytes (or gigabytes) of data.

Remember, if you *do* disable backups for a particular app, the data that you have for that app will no longer be stored in iCloud. So, think carefully before disabling them, to make sure that either you don't really need that data or it's backed up somewhere else.

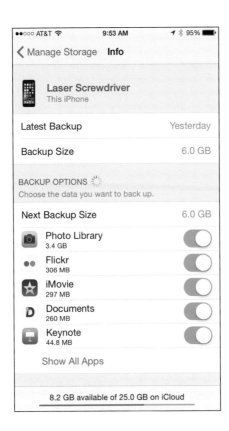

Restoring from Backup

If you're lucky, the only time you might have to restore an iOS device from iCloud Backup is when you get a new device. Fortunately, it's almost as easy as backing up in the first place.

When you launch a fresh phone (or if you've erased your device for trouble-shooting purposes using Erase All Content and Settings under Settings > General > Reset), you're asked if you want to restore from a backup. Choose iCloud Backup to view a list of devices backed up on iCloud, and the date and time of the most recent backup. Select that backup and you're on your way: The iOS device restarts when it's ready to go.

▶ **NOTE** Although iCloud Backup restores your settings, it may not restore all of your passwords, for security reasons. Make sure that you've stored those safely elsewhere, or enable iCloud Keychain (see Chapter 4) to restore them. Alternatively, making encrypted backups to iTunes (see below) will also restore your passwords.

Note that, as mentioned, your apps themselves aren't backed up by this process. Once your phone has been restored, your iOS device automatically re-downloads your apps from the iTunes Store whenever your device is on a Wi-Fi network.

Back Up an iOS Device to iTunes

If you'd rather not back up your iOS device to the cloud, or you want the security of knowing that you've got it backed up in multiple places, you can also make backups to iTunes, via either Wi-Fi, if you've set up iTunes Wi-Fi Sync, or a USB cable. (You can do this even if you don't regularly sync your iOS device to iTunes.)

With your iOS device connected to your Mac, select your device in the toolbar and go to the Backup section (6.4). If you'd like to encrypt your backup, which will preserve all your account passwords, click the Encrypt iPhone Backups checkbox, and then create and verify a password. Click Back Up when you're ready, and then wait while iTunes creates the backup.

6.4 Backing up an iPhone in iTunes

This process is similar to iCloud Backup, with one major exception: If you have media synced via iTunes—including iOS apps—those are additionally backed up. That way, when you restore from the backup, all of that information will make its way across to your iOS device, without having to be re-downloaded via Wi-Fi.

To view which backups are on your Mac, go to iTunes > Preferences and click Devices; you'll see a list of devices and when they were last backed up (6.5). You can delete individual backups—it's a good way to free up space on a drive—but always make sure you keep a current one.

6.5 Checking the amount of storage device backups occupy on disk

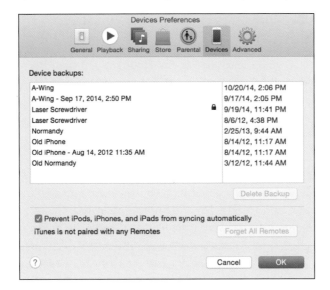

Device backups:

A-Wing	10/20/14, 2:06 PM
A-Wing - Sep 17, 2014, 2:50 PM	9/17/14, 2:05 PM
Laser Screwdriver	9/19/14, 11:41 PM
Laser Screwdriver	8/6/12, 4:38 PM
Normandy	2/25/13, 9:44 AM
Old iPhone	8/14/12, 11:17 AM
Old iPhone - Aug 14, 2012 11:35 AM	8/14/12, 11:17 AM
Old Normandy	3/12/12, 11:44 AM

☑ Prevent iPods, iPhones, and iPads from syncing automatically

iTunes is not paired with any Remotes

Restore from iTunes

Whether you have an erased or fresh device or simply want to restore an older backup onto your iPhone, an iTunes backup is the fastest option.

1. Plug in your device via the USB cable, and click the device icon in the toolbar.

2. If you're restoring a currently working iOS device from backup, skip to step 3. If your device is erased or just out of the box, click the Restore iPhone button to load your most recent backup. That restores the current version of iOS.

3. Choose Restore Backup. If you have more than one backup available, iTunes asks which you'd like to restore from. Your iOS device restarts and begins the restore process.

Back Up a Mac to Time Machine

Backing up your computer used to be a pain, requiring either specialized third-party software or burning DVD after DVD (or CD after CD if you want to go way back, or Zip disk after Zip disk if you really want to dust off those little gray brain cells), and then cataloging those discs so you knew what was where.

But those were in the days before Apple added Time Machine to OS X. The automated backup system greatly simplifies the whole process, and tries to make it much easier not only to set it and forget it, but also to restore files when you need to—even files you've recently deleted.

Back Up Using Time Machine

OS X should prompt you to set up Time Machine when you first configure your Mac, but if you declined or haven't yet activated it, it's easy to do. All you need is a disk on which to back up your data: An external hard drive will do, as will a network drive hooked up to another Mac or a Time Capsule. Fire up System Preferences and click the Time Machine button to open its pane (6.6).

6.6 Time Machine preference pane

As you might guess, enable the system by flipping the big Time Machine switch to On, at which point your Mac prompts you to specify a backup volume from the disks that it can see; you also have the option to set up a Time Capsule if you have one (6.7). If you're worried about someone snooping in your backups, you can also choose to encrypt them if the disk you're selecting supports it.

6.7 Choosing a hard drive to use as a Time Machine backup

Once you've chosen the disk you want to use, Time Machine begins your initial backup, which will probably take some time. From there, it backs up your data every hour. You can also force Time Machine to manually start a backup either by clicking Back Up Now from the Time Machine preference pane or, if you've enabled Time Machine's menu bar icon, by clicking the menu bar icon (6.8).

6.8 Starting a backup from the menu bar

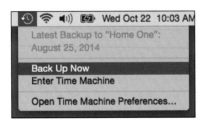

Manage Backups

For the most part, Time Machine backups are self-managing, meaning you shouldn't have to do anything—that's the whole point! The system automatically keeps the last 24 hours of hourly backups, the last month of daily backups, and weekly backups for every month. On a laptop, Time Machine also keeps local snapshots as space allows, letting you recover files even if you're away from your backup disk. If your backup disk begins running out of space, Time Machine prunes the oldest ones first.

One thing you can do if you're concerned about backup space, though, is to exclude certain items from your Time Machine backup. For example, if you use the Dropbox cloud storage service, which instantly syncs and backs up its data, you might decide that it doesn't *also* need to be backed up to Time Machine (although redundancy is a wonderful thing).

To exclude any volume, folder, or file from your Time Machine backup, follow these steps.

1. In the Time Machine pane in System Preferences, click the Options button (6.9).

2. In the sheet that appears, you'll see a list of the items you've told it not to include in backups. To add to the list, click the Add (+) button and navigate to and select the folder, file, or volume.

6.9 Time Machine options

3. If you've changed your mind and decided that an item you previously excluded should be backed up after all, select it from the list and click the Remove (–) button.

4. When you've finished, click Save. Time Machine makes the changes to update your backups accordingly.

If you're concerned about Time Machine cleaning off your old backups, click the checkbox in the Options sheet labeled Notify After Old Backups Are Deleted.

Restore Files

When the unthinkable happens and you lose some data, that's when you turn to Time Machine.

1. Launch Time Machine from the Dock or the Applications folder, or by going to the Time Machine icon in the menu bar and choosing Enter Time Machine.

If you don't have a Finder window open, Time Machine opens one—otherwise it uses the window you're currently looking at. You're presented with a row of copies of the window you're viewing, stretching back into infinity, each representing a single backup (6.10). On the right side of the screen, a timeline documents all of your past backups, and a pair of arrows lets you page through them.

6.10 The Time Machine interface stretching back into the past

2. Locate the file or folder you wish to restore, using any of several options. Click the back arrow to be taken to the last time the contents of the folder you're viewing changed. If you know the exact date of the backup you're looking for, you can also mouse over the timeline on the right-hand side of the screen; as you do, specific dates will pop out. When you find the right one, click it and you'll be shown the folder for that date.

   The Finder window you use in Time Machine is more or less fully functional, letting you switch views or navigate through your hard drive. You can move up and down in the folder hierarchy, select items from the sidebar, use the Search field, and more. In fact, you can even use Quick Look to view a file's contents while in Time Machine, playing back video and audio if appropriate.

3. When you locate the files or folder you want to restore, select them in the Finder window and click the Restore button. You're zipped back to the present, and the files or folders you restored are copied back to their original position. If you try to restore a file whose enclosing folder has been since deleted, Time Machine prompts you to either place the file in a new location or re-create the enclosing folders (6.11).

The enclosing folder for "00 Read First.pdf" no longer exists at its original location. You can recreate the enclosing folder, or choose a new location for the restore.

Cancel   Choose Location...   Recreate Enclosing Folders

6.11 Recreating the old folder structure where needed

Time Machine also works in certain apps, such as Contacts and Mail. If you made a change to a contact record or your mailbox that you want to undo, launch the appropriate app, choose Enter Time Machine from the menu bar icon, and search the same parade of backups for that app in the place of the Finder; just as before, flip back in time and restore an older version.

Restore Your Mac from Time Machine

Should the time come when you need to restore your entire backup from Time Machine—or want to migrate a new Mac from an older one—rest assured that the process isn't terribly difficult. It is time-consuming, though, which is why we recommend that you also have a bootable backup (discussed next).

If you're restoring a Mac from Time Machine, you want to boot up in either Recovery Mode or Internet Recovery mode: Restart your Mac by pressing Command-R or Command-Option-R, respectively. (The only difference between the two modes is that Recovery uses a local partition created by OS X, whereas Internet Recovery requires a network connection to boot remotely; Internet Recovery is best used as a fallback if the Recovery partition has been erased or is otherwise damaged.)

Once you've booted into Recovery mode, you'll have the option to restore your entire disk from your Time Machine backup (assuming, of course, that your backup drive is currently connected to your Mac or available on your network). Choose the date and time of the backup you want to use, and OS X does the heavy lifting of restoring all your files. When it's done, your Mac should reboot, and you should be able to pick up right where your backup left off.

Make Bootable Mac Backups

Time Machine is fine and dandy, but when it comes to backups, redundancy is your friend. And if you suffer a hard disk crash, you want to get up and running right now, without waiting for a lengthy restore process. One additional option to enhance your backup strategy is to create a bootable duplicate of your system using an app such as Shirt Pocket's SuperDuper (shirt-pocket.com). (Other applications perform similarly, such as Bombich Software's Carbon Copy Cloner; www.bombich.com.)

What sets an app like this apart from Time Machine is that it makes an exact clone of your hard drive that you can use to start up and power your computer. If disaster strikes, you can plug in your backup and start your

Mac up from it, getting back to work immediately. Later, at your leisure, you can then clone your backup back to your Mac's drive. It also gives you another copy of your data.

Create a SuperDuper Backup

To use SuperDuper, all you need is an external drive large enough to contain your Mac's startup drive. Connect the drive and launch the application.

1. Using its simple dropdown menus, select the source of the copy—generally your Mac's startup drive—and then the destination (the drive you just connected) (6.12).

6.12 SuperDuper!

2. Choose the method of backing up from the Using dropdown menu. Backup – All Files copies all files on the disk to create a bootable clone; Backup – User Files simply backs up just the files in your user directory.

3. Click the Copy Now button to start. You may need to also enter an administrator's password.

SuperDuper can make and restore backups even without a license, but the $27.95 full version unlocks some really handy features, including the ability to schedule backups. For example, you could make a clone of your startup drive every day at 3 a.m. when you're—hopefully—sound asleep in bed (6.13). That way you never have to worry about your backup being up to date.

6.13 Scheduled copies, the key to worry-free duplicates

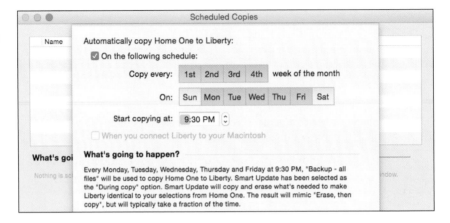

The full version also offers Smart Update, a feature that backs up only those files that have changed since your last backup to that drive. The backup occurs much faster, since fewer files have to be transferred.

▶ **NOTE** Even if you do have an automated backup system, one very important step is *verifying* your backups. If the backup drive goes bad, you don't want to wait to find out when you try to restore it. At least once a month (and possibly more frequently), try starting up your Mac from the Super Duper clone: Go to the Startup Disk preference pane, choose your backup drive, and then click the Restart button (6.14).

6.14 Starting up from the bootable duplicate

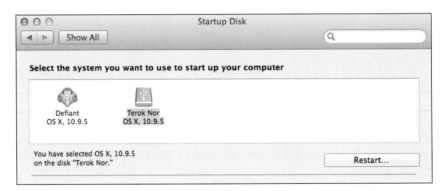

Should you need to restore from your SuperDuper clone, the process works much the same as backing up, just in reverse.

1. Boot your Mac from the clone by using the Startup Disk pane; or, if you can't get your Mac to boot at all, hold the Option key when starting up and select your backup drive.

2. Once the system has booted, launch SuperDuper.

3. Choose your backup drive as the source and your Mac's drive as the destination.

4. Choose the Restore – All Files option from the Using dropdown menu.

5. Click the Copy Now button.

Power users will find a lot of other useful options in SuperDuper, including the ability to run scripts before or after copies, edit the backup scripts themselves, and more.

Offsite Backups

You've got a Time Machine backup. Good. You're running daily clones to SuperDuper. Great! But, as you may expect, your backup strategy isn't complete yet.

What do both your Time Machine backup and your SuperDuper clone have in common? They're likely both in your home. Which means they're both susceptible to disasters like a hurricane, flood, or fire. To truly ensure that your data is always safe, you need an offsite backup.

Disk Swapping

"Offsite backup" may sound like something network administrators talk about in their spare time, but it can be as simple (and cheap) as making a SuperDuper clone once a week or month that you then leave at the office or at a friend or family member's house. Even better is to set up an exchange with a friend or family member, where you hold onto their backup disk and they hold onto yours. You can also store offsite backups in a safe-deposit box or other secure location.

That approach is great if you're diligent about it, but real life has a way of intervening, and some of us simply prefer not to have to think about it. Fortunately, with the wide proliferation of fast Internet, there are lots of great options for automatically backing up your Mac (or Macs) over a network to a remote server.

> **NOTE** Ideally, you have all the components in this chapter set up as a complete backup system. A Time Machine backup records incremental changes in your data; a bootable backup provides a way to get back on your feet quickly; an offsite backup protects against local disaster; and iOS backups keep the data on your devices safe. It sounds extensive, we know, but having multiple backups is so worth it when faced with losing, say, every digital photo you've captured during the last several years.

CrashPlan

Several services allow you to back up all your files to a company's servers. CrashPlan (www.crashplan.com) is among the ones that we really like, because it provides a number of ways to handle remote backups and can accommodate multiple Macs with ease. Other popular options include Backblaze (www.backblaze.com) and Carbonite (www.carbonite.com).

One of CrashPlan's most basic options, which is available for free, is to set up a deal with a family member or friend, like the aforementioned suggestions about storing drives remotely. But instead of having to physically meet and exchange backup drives, you can both install the CrashPlan app on your computers and back up your files across the Internet to the other's computer (or even to a drive that you leave at their house, assuming it's available to a computer on which CrashPlan is installed). And because CrashPlan can be throttled to use only a small amount of bandwidth and even do its backing up during off hours, it won't tax your network connections.

But you can also use CrashPlan to back up all your files to the company's servers, where they're stored safely and with secure encryption. This method requires a subscription to CrashPlan+, which starts at $4 a month for a four-year subscription covering a single computer. But, if you've got a bunch of computers in your household, you can also opt for a subscription that covers between two and ten computers—which ought to account for a pretty solid chunk of your family unit—that starts at $9 a month for a four-year subscription. (The monthly price does go up if you choose a shorter-term subscription.)

Set up CrashPlan

To set up CrashPlan, download and install the app from the company's Web site, then fire it up. Create a user account (or log in to an existing account), after which you can choose what backup method—or methods—you want to use (6.15). Aside from backing up to a friend's computer or CrashPlan's servers, you can also have your files copied to another computer you own or to a specific folder somewhere—both of which are available in the free version of CrashPlan.

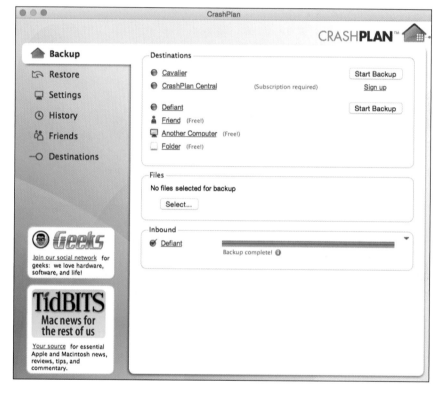

6.15 CrashPlan backup methods

If you're backing up over the network, be aware that the initial backup may take a pretty long time—we're talking hours, days, perhaps even weeks, depending on how much data you're backing up. CrashPlan throttles its traffic so it doesn't overwhelm your network connection, which means that it backs up pretty slowly. You can tweak how much CPU and bandwidth it uses, both when you're at the computer and when the computer is idle, in the app's Settings section (6.16, on the next page).

6.16 Control how much of the Mac's CPU is used for backups.

If you've got a lot of data—300 GB or more—you can kickstart the process by using CrashPlan's optional Seeded Backup service. The company sends you a drive that you can fill with your data and then send back to it; then you only have to make incremental backups. You'll need to be a subscriber to take advantage of it.

The great part about CrashPlan and similar services is that once you set them up, you can more or less forget about them until you need them. They'll take care of all the hassle of automatically backing up your files and verifying them. CrashPlan also lets you quickly and easily restore specific files from your backups, à la Time Machine (6.17). And if you migrate to a new computer, you can use the Adopt option to migrate your existing backup to your replacement machine.

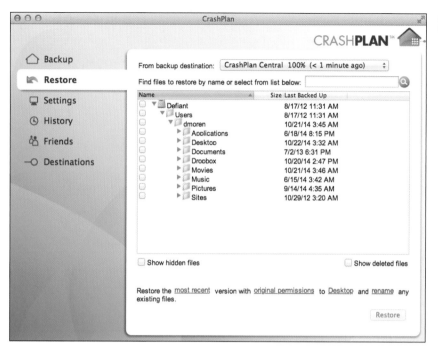

6.17 Restoring from a CrashPlan backup

Dropbox

If you're less concerned with backing up your entire computer online than simply ensuring that your most important files stay secure and safe, consider turning to a service like Dropbox. While many individuals and organizations take advantage of the cloud-storage service to keep their files in sync across multiple computers, it can also be a handy way to maintain backups.

When you install Dropbox, it creates a special folder in the home directory of your Mac, called, appropriately, Dropbox (6.18, on the next page). Any files in this folder are automatically synced to other computers you own that are also logged in to Dropbox, but the files are also stored on Dropbox's own servers, where you can access them via a Web interface.

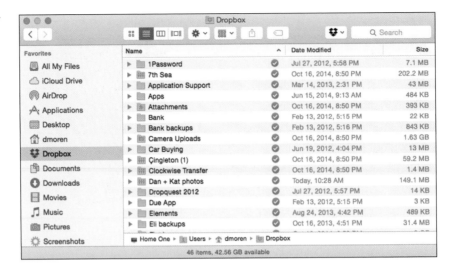

Though Dropbox is primarily concerned with keeping your files in sync across multiple machines, it also maintains a history of files you stored. Via the Web interface, you can view files that have been deleted and undelete any that were erased by mistake (6.19).

6.19 The contents of your Dropbox folder on the Web

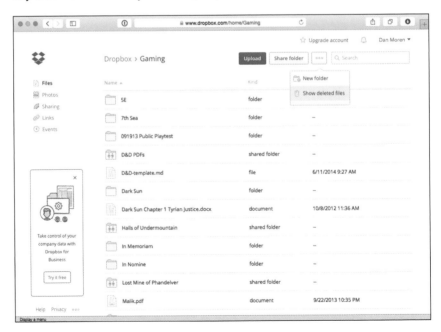

Dropbox also stores multiple versions of files: when you're in the Web interface, Control-click any file and select Previous Versions and you'll see a full history of all the changes made to that file, along with timestamps, file sizes, and more (6.20). Clicking any of the previous versions lets you preview that version of the file; you can restore that version by selecting it and then clicking Restore at the bottom.

Because of the way Dropbox works, it's not really sufficient for backing up your entire computer, but if you just want to avoid accidentally deleting some files (or make sure that your work is available wherever you go), it's a pretty good solution. You can sign up for a free account that gets you 2GB of storage, but a paid option can jump that up to 1TB—enough to store pretty much all of your critical files.

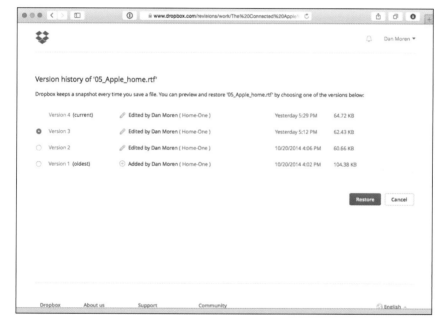

6.20 Browsing the version history of a file at the Dropbox site

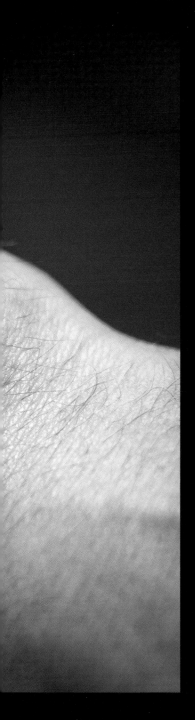

CHAPTER 7

The Apple Future

As you can imagine, the company that created the iPhone isn't stopping the pursuit to find new methods for its devices to communicate. iOS is built on the same core OS X technology that runs Macs, and now Apple is extending that to new products like the Apple Watch. With software frameworks such as HealthKit and HomeKit for developers, Apple has also opened up iOS and OS X to other companies who want to build devices that tie into the Apple ecosystem.

As we write this, however, we're just on the cusp of these developments. Apple introduced the Apple Watch with much fanfare, but it's not expected to ship until sometime in 2015. And although HealthKit and HomeKit arrived with iOS 8 and OS X Yosemite, only the first trickle of products is starting to arrive. We anticipate there will be more when you're reading this.

So, based on what we know so far, here's a peek into the Apple near-future to see how the Mac, iPhone, iPad, iPod touch, and Apple TV are expected to work with new products.

The Apple Watch

The Apple Watch is the company's most interconnected product: Although it can do plenty on its own, it benefits greatly from connecting wirelessly with an iPhone.

Communicate

How many times do you pull your iPhone out of a pocket or bag just to check the time? Or respond to texts? The beauty of a watch is the ability to glance at it discreetly to quickly get information. Taking advantage of the Continuity features introduced in OS X Yosemite and iOS 8, the Apple Watch will display incoming phone call information, displaying caller ID for numbers that are in your list of contacts. You can answer and take the call on your wrist, send a text back if you can't pick up, or take the call on the iPhone.

> ▶ **TIP** We love this idea: If a call comes in and you're not able to answer it right away, simply cover the Apple Watch with your other hand to send the caller to voicemail.

When a text message or email message arrives, it appears on the watch's screen. You can tap the touch-sensitive face and reply with preset answers (similar to what the iPhone and iPad offer on the Lock screen when declining a phone call), shoot it back to the iPhone to reply in Messages or Mail, or use Siri to dictate a response.

In fact, Siri becomes an important part of the Apple Watch experience. It's one of the main methods of discovering information, such as checking the weather (7.1).

Perhaps most interesting are the Digital Touch methods of subtly getting the attention of someone else who owns an Apple Watch. Instead of sending text, you can initiate a short walkie-talkie conversation between the watches. Or, you can sketch a little doodle on the watch face, which is sent to the other person's watch. Another option is to send a tap: When you tap the screen, the other person feels a vibration (which can be customized) from the watch's taptic feedback generators on the underside. Those also enable you to send your heartbeat—yes, your current pulse rate.

Essential Information

As a convenient point of reference, the Apple Watch can access your calendars and contacts. With the connection to the iPhone, of course, you can also view maps; if you're using the Maps app to provide directions, the watch can even guide you to your location by activating feedback specific to turning left or right when needed.

What makes us more excited is the ability to use Apple Pay with the Apple Watch to make purchases. As we write this, Apple Pay is available only on the iPhone 6 and iPhone 6 Plus, but the Apple Watch will make it possible to pay for items even if you have an older iPhone. Similarly, the Apple Watch can store loyalty cards and items such as airline tickets using Passbook—just scan your wrist to get onto a plane, into a movie, or to pay for a Starbucks coffee.

Don't forget that the Apple Watch is a timepiece, so it will offer time-related functions such as stopwatch, timer, alarms, and naturally, dozens of watch faces for telling time.

Media

The prospect of watching a movie doesn't appeal on such a small screen (don't worry, Apple has said nothing about a video feature), but other media possibilities will be possible—specifically, using the Apple Watch as a remote control. You can choose which music plays on the iPhone and control the playback, control an Apple TV (no more scrambling to find that little silver remote!), and even use the Apple Watch as a remote camera for the camera in your iPhone.

And for those times when you need to share a photo, you can scroll through and view your photos right on the watch (although we're understandably skeptical that the face size will let you see much).

Fitness

Apple is pushing the Apple Watch as a serious fitness wearable. The sensors on the underside of the watch pick up heart rate (7.2), and the device taps the accelerometer and GPS data in the iPhone for motion data. That information is then tracked, with apps for recording progress, setting goals, and nailing fitness achievements (7.3). (Yes, that means the iPhone must go along when you exercise; the Apple Watch can't do it all.)

7.2 Rear sensors on the Apple Watch

7.3 Tracking fitness info during a workout

Health Apps and Devices

Speaking of fitness, Apple's push into health has already begun with iOS 8. The new Health app is a dashboard for storing motion data, like steps taken, body weight, caloric intake, and other factors that will hopefully help keep you in better shape. Some iPhone apps, such as the calorie-tracker Lose It!, already share data to the Health app. Apple's developer framework, called HealthKit, allows third parties to build that sort of integration into apps and devices. Expect to see new wearables that can talk directly to the Health app using HealthKit.

▶ **TIP** If you own an iPhone with the Health app, do this right now: Open the app, tap the Medical ID button, and enter vital medical conditions and emergency contacts. If something were to happen to you, a bystander or doctor can access this information from the iPhone's locked home screen (swipe to unlock, then tap the Emergency).

Home Apps and Devices

When so many products talk to each other, it's natural to want even more communication among devices, and your home is the next place the conversation will take place. Apple's HomeKit development framework is designed to interact with devices in the home such as lights, doors, thermostats, and other static controls. Using an iOS device, you could set the heat to turn on shortly before you get home, change the lighting in a room, track water and electricity usage, and more.

Products that take advantage of HomeKit should start appearing in 2015.

INDEX

Numbers

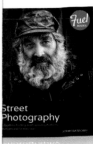